Consecration

to Jesus through

Our Lady of the Blessed Sacrament

Statue of Our Lady of the Blessed Sacrament
St. Jean Baptiste Catholic Church, New York, New York

Consecration

to Jesus through

Our Lady of the Blessed Sacrament

33 Days with Saint Peter Julian Eymard
Apostle of the Eucharist

Laura Catherine Worhacz

Elisheba House
Trinity, FL

To Jesus in the Blessed Sacrament,

who has blessed me with the grace to know Him in the Most Holy Sacrament of the Altar through the heart of the Mother of God, my Mother.

" Try to catch something of her spirit. "

St. Peter Julian Eymard

TABLE OF CONTENTS

Table of Contents

FOREWORD

You hold in your hand a precious gift. In whatever way this book came to you, take a moment right now and welcome it with a prayer. It is a gift offered to you from your mother, Mary. She who is espoused in love with the Holy Spirit brings this work to you through Laura Worhacz' reflections on St. Peter Julian Eymard's writings.

Mary was overshadowed by the *Most High,* in humble obedience to maternity. A fearful request made of her by the angel sent from God of the secret incarnation of divinity in her humanity. She had to sacrifice all she had anticipated for her life and risk the shame of unwed pregnancy. Here begins the Passion of Jesus; from conception Mary is obedient to the will of the Father. In humility as a servant she submits, "May it be done to me according to your word" (Luke 1:38).

The betrothed union of Mary to the Holy Spirit is offered to you in using this book as a method to prepare your consecration to Jesus. Filled with the presence of God in her womb she became the ark of the new covenant. In the birth of her Son she undoes the disobedience of Eve and becomes the mother of a new humanity reborn in Baptism into the eternal life of her Son.

The pages of this book bring you into an intimacy with God waiting to unfold in your life. Through the daily reflections and weekly themes, Laura guides us as we open our hearts to the fullness of God's plan for us. The act of consecration is set in viewing Mary who prefigured and models living the paschal mystery of Jesus. It is from her flesh and blood that He embraces our humanity and in obedience to the Father as beloved Son gives himself in total self-offering his flesh and blood as food to eat and drink, gift of eternal life. In this way we see the Eucharist as the fruit of Mary's womb and our lives as fruit on the vine. *"Whoever remains in me and I in you will bear much fruit, because without me you can do nothing"* (John 15:5).

You have received a gift in your hand that comes from Laura's relationship with the Apostle of the Eucharist, St. Peter Julian Eymard. In this book you will find the writings, sermons and retreat notes of a priest who was on fire with the Eucharist. His passion was to transform the world by making known the depth of God's love made available in a perpetual manner in the Blessed Sacrament. Peter Julian said that Mary's mission is to form Jesus in us.

With his mother's death in his youth he claimed Mary as his mother and thought of himself as her son, to learn from her how to pray and love Jesus in the Eucharist. He attributes his desire to become a priest to Mary and after ordination as a diocesan priest requested leave from his Bishop to join the newly found Society of Mary. While praying at the shrine of Our Lady of Fourviere, Mary lit a fire in his heart to sacrifice everything, to leave everything dear to him in order to establish a new society in the Church; one that would be totally devoted to the divine presence of God in the Blessed Sacrament and would make this sacrament of God's love known throughout the world.

Peter Julian teaches us how Mary realizes in herself the Eucharistic life of Jesus. She was consumed with the desire to inflame all hearts with the love her son offers in his self-giving. Your life will be altered in the celebration of the Mass when you place it with the bread and wine on the altar and have the Holy Spirit overshadow you to transform your life to be centered in the Eucharist. *"As the living Father sent me and I have life because of the Father, so also the one who feeds on me will have life because of me" (John 6:57).*

Know that you are being prayed for as you use this book to prepare for your consecration to Jesus through Our Lady of the Blessed Sacrament. Whoever has an encounter with the Eucharist does not live anymore for oneself but for Jesus. When making his consecration as a *Gift of Self,* Father Eymard heard Jesus speak to him; *"You will be entirely invested with me. My heart will beat within our body; my soul will act through your soul. Your heart will be the receptacle and the pulsation of my heart. I shall be the person of your personality, and your personality will be the life of my person in you."* (March 21, 1865).

Rev. William Fickel, SSS
Pastor, St. Vincent de Paul Catholic Church
Holiday, FL

2/11/19
Feast of Our Lady of Lourdes

MARY GATHERS HER CHILDREN

In gratitude to the Mother of God, Our Lady of the Most Blessed Sacrament, your intentions are ours. Special thanks to:

- ❖ Ivonne and Rick Hernandez, for working so closely with me throughout this project. This work would not have been provided in the manner it is presented if it was not for their collaboration and support, from its conception in the Elisheba Blog until its final publishing. Our friendship has been blessed.
- ❖ Reverend Father William Fickel, SSS, whose encouragement brought life to this work. The attentiveness Father William offered this project, and the trust he valued in Jesus Eucharistic creating the consecration through me was a gift beyond description. "Grant us continual growth in holiness under the direction of our pastors."[1]

---

[1] Common of Pastors/Office of readings, Christian Prayer.

❖ The Congregation of the Blessed Sacrament, for their life and mission to make the love of God known in the Eucharist.

❖ Jim Brown, Director of the Center for Eucharistic Evangelizing (CEE), and Father Paul Bernier, SSS, for their help with the editing of the Introduction.

❖ The Associates of the Blessed Sacrament around the globe, who share in the mission and the charism of our spiritual father, St. Peter Julian Eymard.

❖ The Mothers of the Blessed Sacrament prayer cenacle, my sisters in Christ, who have consecrated their life to Jesus through Our Lady of the Most Blessed Sacrament.

❖ My family, my husband Raymond and the children God Blessed us with, Nicole and Mary. The greatest grace for us continues to be our faith in God, our love for His Son in the Blessed Sacrament and the gift of Mary, our Mother. Our daughters are the light of our lives in Christ. Thank you, Nicole, for your help with the editing of the reflections.

❖ St. Peter Julian Eymard, who, through his spiritual writings, directs souls that come to him.

And, above all, eternally grateful to JESUS CHRIST truly present in the Blessed Sacrament, who has blessed us with His Divine Life and the gift of His Mother, the Strong One!

It is with great joy that I invite you to participate in this consecration preparation. This life changing experience will daily nourish your journey of faith through our Eucharistic Lord and the heart of our Mother.

Laura Catherine Worhacz

INTRODUCTION

Consecration

To consecrate oneself to Jesus Christ through Our Lady of the Blessed Sacrament is to desire a life of holiness, to be set apart for a sacred purpose in God Our Father's love. This book should be for you a lifelong companion, never to be filed away. The prayers included in this consecration preparation should become part of your daily prayers forever. This consecration preparation, inspired by the Holy Spirit, interweaves St. Peter Julian's great Marian love with what it means to be a consecrated child of God. In the pages of this book you will discover how to prepare to consecrate your life and how to live each day after your consecration promise. We give our lives, our wills, our entire being to Jesus Christ through our Lady of the Blessed Sacrament. This is what it means to consecrate oneself. It is my hope that the impeccable love St. Peter Julian Eymard has for Our Blessed Mother will be passed onto the beloved children of God who seek to find a deeper Eucharistic union with Jesus and Mary.

To Jesus

Jesus is the Bread of Life. He invites us to make him the center of our lives. We live in the risen Lord when we live in the Holy Eucharist. This is our faith, our Catholic faith. We are never alone. We are born into the family of God by our Baptism in Christ, renewed by our participation in the sacraments. God the Father has not only blessed his children with his Son to redeem us from the corruption of original sin, He gave us a MOTHER! The greatest gift after Jesus in the Blessed Sacrament is a dedicated faithful relationship with the Blessed Virgin Mary, Mother of God. Like any relationship, it needs to be nourished to be healthy. With great hope this method of preparation will bring you closer to our Eucharistic Lord.

Through Mary

Our Blessed Mother was privileged to bring the Son of God into the world. Our Father could have chosen many ways to send Jesus to us. God very significantly brought Jesus Christ into the world through Mary, who was the first tabernacle and adorer of the Incarnate Word.

Mary was the first adorer and the first member of the Body of Christ. In the Immaculate Conception they were one from the beginning. There was never a separation. Jesus entered Mary's womb at the Annunciation to become incarnate in her. He was born into the world through her, and she remained one with him. Jesus came from her body and Mary remained in His mystical body by her life of worshiping her son in mind and heart.

Mary's humble "Yes" to God was our entrance into the mercy of God. Mary received the Body of Christ that came down from Heaven when she conceived Jesus at the announcement of Gabriel, "Let it be done unto me according to your WORD!"

With Saint Peter Julian Eymard

St. Peter Julian Eymard was canonized during the Second Vatican Council on December 9, 1962 by St. Pope John, XXIII, and given the title, *Apostle of the Eucharist*. St. Peter Julian believed that Mary, the Mother of God, brought him to Jesus in the Eucharist. From that moment on, he lived his life in the Eucharist. His love for the Blessed Mother and his relationship with her helped St. Peter Julian establish the Congregation of the Blessed Sacrament.

The Congregation is composed of religious priests and brothers, Sister Servants and lay Associates throughout the world. They make up the one Eymardian family, entrusted with promoting and protecting the Eucharistic charism St. Peter Julian left the Catholic Church.

This Outstanding Apostle of the Eucharist blessed the Church with the most magnificent title for Mary—OUR LADY OF THE BLESSED SACRAMENT. The charism of St. Peter Julian Eymard held the fire of God's love alive in his heart by the faithful dedication to Jesus in the Holy Eucharist. St. Peter Julian's love lives through the lives of his daughters and sons when we celebrate the mystery of the Eucharist worthily, adore Jesus Christ truly present in the Blessed Sacrament and proclaim it prophetically for God's greater glory.

33 Days

This book, inspired by the charism of St. Peter Julian Eymard, will serve as a method of preparation to consecrate oneself to Jesus Christ through Our Lady of the Most Blessed Sacrament. The excerpts found at the beginning of each day are taken from Volume 7 of the Eymard Library, *Our Lady of the Blessed Sacrament.*[2] The daily readings, meditations and prayers should bring us to an ever-greater awareness that we live in the presence of the living God. Jesus Christ, truly present in the Blessed Sacrament, is where Our Lady of the Blessed Sacrament will take us. The process to prepare involves 33 days. It is symbolic of the number of years Jesus spent on earth. We consecrate our lives to Jesus who remains with us in the Paschal Mystery.

Through original sin we are enfeebled and weakened. With Jesus Christ living in us we are strong. St. Peter Julian calls Mary, "O Thou Strong One!"[3] We need this strong one to be by our side every minute of our days. Consecrating oneself to Jesus Christ through Mary is a lifelong dedication and way of life in the Eucharist. We do not file it away, ever. We live it forever!

This book will serve you as a great treasure. You will never be without the Blessed Virgin Mary, Mother of God by your side. Your consecration promise will be etched in your heart by the faith you place into it. With hope you will draw

---

[2] There is a nine-volume series of books referred to as the Eymard Library. It was compiled and published after Father Eymard's death by Father Albert Tesniere, SSS.

[3] Peter Julian Eymard, *Our Lady of the Blessed Sacrament*, (Ohio, Emmanuel, 1930), 95.

closer and closer to Jesus Eucharistic and long to receive Him, even daily, for Holy Communion is food for our spiritual journey; our strength is in God's grace. Grace can be received in many ways, however, the Holy Sacrifice of the Mass, the highest form of prayer, will grant you many blessings. If you cannot receive Jesus daily, perhaps take away from this promise the practice of making a daily Spiritual Communion.

The Annunciation of the Lord to Mary (March 25th) is an ideal time to conclude the 33 days of preparation to consecrate your life to Jesus through Our Lady of Most Blessed Sacrament. This great Solemnity is when the "Word became flesh and dwelt among us" (John 1:4). It is Mary's "Yes" to become the mother of Jesus, to help redeem the world by Jesus Christ becoming incarnate in her womb.

We too are invited to have the Body of Christ, the living God, incarnate in us. We strive for this by the way of Mary, for she was the first to live with Jesus incarnate. She will lead us our whole life long with the desire to stay close to the holy Eucharist. Our good Mother knows we need the nourishment for our souls. We die without JESUS.

If you choose another Marian or Saint's feast day to conclude your consecration that is perfectly fine; simply begin 33 days prior to the day you choose. Once you have made your consecration it would be advisable to renew your promise on special days. You may choose to recite the prayer to Our Lady of the Blessed Sacrament daily as a holy reminder of your consecration promise, it should always bring you to the Blessed Sacrament as a grateful adorer of Jesus Christ.

Living the Consecration

As a consecrated child of God, it should become natural for us to long to return our love to God the Father, God the Son and God the Holy Spirit. Walking with Mary in all we do will help guide our lives. We will want to bring witness to our love for Jesus through Our Lady. We will make Marian feast days special, especially May 13, when we celebrate Our Lady of the Most Blessed Sacrament in the Catholic Church. We will long to bring others into relationship with our Mother whom we love.

Remember the words of St. Peter Julian Eymard, "Try to catch something of her spirit."[4]

It is my hope that this consecration preparation will be a fruitful spiritual experience of surrendering your will over to the will of God, making Him the center of your life, entering a life of union with God through prayer, love and ultimately, service. We, Mary's consecrated, are given the greater awareness that we are helping her in leading God's children back to him.

Jesus Christ, the redeemer of humanity, remains with us in the Bread of Life that has come down from Heaven. He remains with us for the salvation of all. Our lives must conform to the life of Jesus Christ truly present in the Blessed Sacrament. Our mission is to bring all to the Holy Eucharist to heal a suffering world.

St. Peter Julian Eymard will bless you with his love for Our Blessed Mother. Mary played such an important role in his life, even inspiring him to found the Congregation of the

---

[4] Ibid., 94.

Blessed Sacrament. The work of Jesus Eucharistic was made manifest in his life. With the guidance of St. Peter Julian through the heart of Mary, may this method of preparation to consecrate your life to Jesus through Our Lady of the Most Blessed Sacrament forever keep you in the presence of God.

How to Use This Book

- **Choose your Consecration Day**

  Prayerfully choose a day of significance to you (i.e. an anniversary, birthday, Marian feast day, Saint's feast day) to recite your consecration promise. You will want to renew this promise annually, setting aside the same 33-day period to prepare.

  Begin the readings for **Week1–Day1** thirty-three days before the date you would like to complete the preparation and recite the consecration promise.

  For example, if you choose the Solemnity of the Annunciation of the Lord (March 25th) as the day to conclude your consecration preparation, you will begin the readings for **Week1-Day1** on February 20th.

- **Before you begin**

  There are seven Preparatory Meditations to help you enter more deeply into this spiritual exercise. You may take a week to go through them, reading one each day, or you may read them all at once.

- **Establish a time to pray**

  Be obedient to your prayer routine. Set aside ten minutes each day for this consecration preparation, preferably in the morning. There are some weeks with brief readings and some with longer ones. Take some time to meditate on what you have read. Journal through the process; this is your conversation with God, listening, praying and responding.

  If you fall behind on your readings, just read when you are able (even if it is after reciting your consecration promise). Let nothing stop you from participating in this consecration to Jesus through Our Lady of the Most Blessed Sacrament.

- **Daily Prayers in Appendix A**

  Each week has prayers listed to accompany the daily readings. The prayers can be found in Appendix A at the end of the book.

- **Prepare for a good Confession (to be offered before reciting your consecration promise)**

  May the Holy Spirit fill you with every grace and blessing in the fulfillment of the Promise of Our Heavenly Father.

Preparatory Meditations

The Incarnation

Mary's consent to the Incarnation inaugurates the great mystery of reparation to God and union with us which Jesus Christ accomplished during His mortal life, and that He continues in the Eucharist.[5]- St. Peter Julian

The Incarnation, the Annunciation, is the most pivotal moment in the history of man. This is when the promise of the Father is given to us by way of Mary. Through Mary's yes, Her Fiat, the triumph over sin and death became a reality for us. It is written, "And you shall conceive and bear a Son, and His name shall be called Jesus" (Luke 1:31-33).

We consecrate as simple children of God offering back to Him His life in us. We keep the Incarnation of Jesus Christ alive through our Baptism and the reception of Holy Communion. Our fallen human nature rises through the redeeming life of Jesus Christ offered to us in the Blessed Sacrament.

---

[5] Eymard, *Our Lady of the Blessed Sacrament*, 1.

Behold Thy Mother

We are obliged to, in order to continue in the grace of our vocation and participate fully in it, to give very special honor to the Blessed Virgin under the title of Our Lady of the Most Blessed Sacrament.

Without Mary, we shall never find Jesus, for she possesses Him in her heart. We must never separate Jesus from Mary; we can go to Him only through her. Our Lord owes everything through her in the order of His Incarnation.[6]- St. Peter Julian

These are strong statements of truth for those who believe! For those who do not understand the gift or our Blessed Mother, let us pray that the fullness of the Holy Spirit may be upon them.

God sent His Son by way of Mary very significantly and specifically. The human family in the natural order of life needs a mother. Life is better with a mother. The comfort, the guidance, the gifts that come from a mother are without end. At the foot of the cross our Lord gave us Mary, He said, "Behold thy mother" (John 19:27). We have a spiritual mother who brings us to the Son of God. There is no separation between the two.

In the excerpt above, St. Peter Julian tells us that the Incarnation makes Jesus and Mary one. Mary received Jesus in her womb; she bore Him into the world through the fullness of

---

[6] Ibid., 2.

the Holy Spirit, the Promise of the Father.[7] She was made one with Him by receiving the Body of Christ. We receive them both by our own reception of Holy Communion. Through Jesus in the Holy Trinity and Mary as the first entry into the Body, we are all part of the Mystical Body of Christ. The Father could have sent Jesus down from above in many ways, yet He knew our human needs and fulfilled them through the gift of motherhood.

Without time and effort, a relationship remains unnourished; we are blessed to renew our thanks for having a Mother through the Eucharist. Our human frailty is greatly restored by the reception of Holy Communion, for it is by the Incarnation of Christ living in and through our own lives in the womb of Mary that we are renewed.

Our Lady of the Blessed Sacrament

And devotion to our Lady of the Most Blessed Sacrament will grow with the worship of the Eucharist. I have not found this devotion treated of in any work; nor have I ever heard it spoken of except in the Revelations of Mother Mary of Jesus, where I read something about Mary's Communions; and again, in the Acts of the Apostles, where we find our Lady in the Cenacle.

She was the Mother and Queen of adorers. She was in a word, Our Lady of the Most Blessed Sacrament.[8] - St. Peter Julian

---

[7] When you see "The Promise of the Father" throughout the book, think of the Holy Spirit.

[8] Eymard, *Our Lady of the Blessed Sacrament*, 5.

In the preparatory meditations special emphasis should be given to what is being said by St. Peter Julian. After the crucifixion Mary lived some 20 years. Mary's fiat united her heart to the cenacle.[9] Through her own reception of Holy Communion, the resurrection of her Son was kept alive; it pierced through the sorrow of Calvary. Until the Assumption, the Apostle St. John celebrated Mass for Mary so that she could receive Jesus in the Blessed Sacrament.

A Promise

All her virtues bore the Eucharistic stamp. Let us ask our Lord what passed between Him and His Blessed Mother during those years in the Cenacle. He will make known to us some of these wonders. One must understand, furthermore, the thanksgiving of Mary's love. The essential thing is to try to practice some given virtue of the Blessed Virgin's. Begin at once with the lowest, the smallest of these. When you have made them your own, your will go on, little by little, till you come to her interior virtues, even to that of her love. Then let us offer up some sacrifice.[10] - St. Peter Julian

The vow that we are taking in participating in this consecration summons the reality of the promise we are making to God. A vow is a free and deliberate promise made to God for a good work. This act belongs to the virtue of

---

[9] When you see the word *cenacle*, think of the gathering place, the Upper Room, the Altar of the Lord, and our hearts connected there during the consecration at holy Mass.

[10] Eymard, *Our Lady of the Blessed Sacrament*, 7.

religion, acknowledging the supreme dominion of God, and professing our submission to Him.[11] The Promise of the Father in His gifts of the spirit will be given to us if we stay close to His Son in the Blessed Sacrament. The question above, "what passed between Him and His Blessed Mother?", can be applied to our own lives. In answer, St. Peter Julian recommends sacrifice. Love is reciprocal, it calls for a return, so if love is a sacrifice we need to offer something in return to God. We begin by examining the disposition of our hearts. We think of the purity of our intentions, we think of our concern for others, but most importantly, we remember the love that was poured out for us from the Cross. When the reality of this love enters our soul amidst the crosses, toils, and disappointments of life, the gift of thanksgiving is left for us.

"He will make know to us some of these wonders."[12] St. Peter Julian

The wonderment of hope will increasingly grow in our lives by clinging to Mary through her virtues.

Children of Mary

Let us be in short, but Mary's shadow. A sacrifice anticipated makes us reason, and reasoning diminishes its merit; but those that we accept generously without premeditation or deliberation are of more value. God wants to surprise us. Hold thyself in readiness! Let us never lose the opportunity to sacrifice; all that is necessary is to be generous. Let us offer all her actions, all her

---

[11] https://www.catholicculture.org/culture/library/dictionary/index.cfm?id=37146.
[12] Eymard, *Our Lady of the Blessed Sacrament*, 7.

merits, all her virtues to our Lord. We have only to have recourse to Mary and to say to Jesus: "I offer Thee the riches that my good Mother has acquired for me" -and our Lord will be very much pleased with us.[13]- St. Peter Julian

To be in Mary's shadow we must emulate her ways. To be ready to sacrifice we must do what she does. Mary's ways are God's ways. Throughout her whole life, she was ready to sacrifice. "My ways are higher than your ways, and my thoughts than your thoughts" (Isaiah 55:9).

As children of Mary, we enter into the consecration days. Let us remember that just as the Holy Spirit overshadowed our Blessed Mother, we must empty ourselves to let the Holy Spirit overshadow us. In this relationship with the Holy Spirit of God's Love, we prepare for prayer. The consecration is a prayer, given by our Father, to be born of our Mother, to grab hold of her hand and walk through our lives.

There are many ways of prayer. Let the Holy Spirit guide you through this method of preparation to consecrate your life to Jesus Christ, ultimately finding our Lord truly present in the Blessed Sacrament. We do this with a conscious effort not only to recognize Jesus in the breaking of the bread, but also to enter into His Divine Love. This is the life Mary lived; His Love permeated throughout her life. She was ready for any sacrifice; the ultimate sacrifice being standing in the shadow of the Cross of her Son. Mary would never have had this readiness of spirit if she was not beheld in The Promise of the Father, in His gifts of the Holy Spirit.

---

[13] Ibid., 8.

Empty Thyself

O Glorious Chaplain of the cenacle, you will teach us to know the mysteries of the life of our Lady of the Most Blessed Sacrament; you will make us enter into her dispositions every time we receive or adore the God of the Eucharist. We need a model, a patron, a guide in our devotion to Our Lady of the Most Blessed Sacrament. We choose St. John the Evangelist. Jesus had entrusted His Mother to him, and St. John celebrated Holy Mass daily in the presence of Mary. St. John was the witness of Mary's Adoration; he was the confidant of her love. not only that he might be a son to her in His place, but that he might by the Holy Mysteries he celebrated for her, and according to her intentions, give her the means of satisfying her heart's ardent desires for the establishment of the Church, and also to console her for her Son's absence by the happiness she felt in being nourished with Him every day.[14] - St. Peter Julian

---

Are we not all drawn to be like the beloved disciple who rested his head on the Heart of Jesus Christ at the Last Supper? Mary, teach us to pray.

We pray to empty ourselves and let the Holy Spirit enter our hearts, minds, bodies, and souls. God chose to leave Our Lady on earth after His Crucifixion for over twenty years. This was yet another gift for us. "Then he said to the disciple, 'Behold, your mother.' And from that hour the disciple took her into his home" (John 19:27). Mary continued to live her life in God after the Crucifixion of Her Son. St. John served her

---

[14] Ibid., 9.

Holy Communion as he celebrated Holy Mass daily. The love of Jesus was brought down from Heaven "to give her the means to satisfy her hearts desires for the establishment of the Church."[15]

We too are invited to receive Jesus in Holy Communion with the desire to further establish the Catholic Church throughout our lives. The eagle represents St. John. He soars above all things by keeping his head resting on the Heart of Jesus Christ at the Last Supper. He is the beloved disciple, the faithful one who stood at the foot of the cross. May this faithfulness be ours through the intercession of St. John, the glorious chaplain of the Cenacle. May he bring us to Mary and help us behold Her as Mother.

It is Forever

St. Peter Julian Eymard writes in a letter, Holy Thursday April 9th, 1846 to Sister Marguerite Guillot:[16]

I want to get this letter out of the way, my daughter, with these few lines. I'm sorry that I didn't give you permission on Tuesday to keep company with our good Master on Thursday night - he who is alone, sad and suffering at the grotto of the Mount of Olives. I grant it to you willingly and would even wish to be able to go with you. Then, Easter day is coming, that beautiful day which dries every tear, and restores Jesus to us so beautiful and gracious. So, I must also give you back to the good Father, and

---

[15] Ibid.

[16] As an interesting note, April 9th, 2018 was the Solemnity of the Annunciation, and thus the Consecration Promise Day for that year for those who were joining us through the Elisheba Blog.

give you a bouquet for his tender Mother. So, here it is; I am permitting you to consecrate yourself by a special vow to Mary who is so pure and gracious making her your custodian, your protectress, in a word, your Mistress of Novices. My poor daughter, can I give you anyone better? Oh! How fortunate you are! It's reason enough to cry for joy. Our Lord will be so pleased to communicate his graces through Mary's heart, to speak to you and show himself to you there. By this vow you will go to Jesus through Mary. You will love Jesus in the arms of Mary. When our beloved Savior calls you to the foot of his cross, you will find Mary there. She is already your Mother, she will be doubly so. Oh, it seems to me that this vow of holy slavery will obtain many graces for you and much love.

It's understood that when we vow ourselves to the Queen of Heaven and Earth in this manner, it is forever. Please tell her also that I am her humble son. Take heart! On Sunday you will say: "I have died, but my life is hidden with Jesus and Mary in God." . . . All yours in our Lord, Eymard[17]

In consecrating your life to Jesus through our Lady of the Most Blessed Sacrament, St. Peter Julian Eymard enlightens us to the reality that it is forever.

The above letter to Sister Marguerite from St. Peter Julian Eymard should be read a few times and very slowly. The account of these words written contain everything necessary to enter into this spiritual journey.

---

[17] Peter Julian Eymard, SSS, translated by Catherine Marie Caron, SSS, *The Life and Letters of Saint Peter Julian Eymard, Volume 1 The Early Years 1828-1852,* (Cleveland, Congregation of the Blessed Sacrament,1990), 98.

WEEK ONE

THEME: MARY, TEACH US THE LIFE OF ADORATION

Intention this week:

Pray through the intercession of Our Lady of the Blessed Sacrament. If you cannot get to Daily Mass, you can offer a spiritual communion prayer. The faith you place into it will be the grace you receive back. Keep a journal.

May this preparation to consecrate your life to Jesus Christ be a time to offer sacrifices in the hope of rising closer to God.

Prayers for each day this week (found in Appendix A)

- Veni Creator
- Ave Maris Stella

Week 1 - Day 1

Mary, Mother of Eucharistic Adorers

Jesus is the King of the Eucharist, and He wishes only trained servitors in His court, only those who have served their apprenticeship. One must learn to serve before presenting oneself to the King. All Mary's life -taken as a whole- may be summed up in this one word-adoration; for adoration is the perfect service of God, and it embraces all the duties of the creature toward the Creator.[18] - St. Peter Julian

Mary lived a life of perpetual giving, perpetual offering, and perpetual serving. Mary's life was filled with a never-ending gift of herself to God; it pleased her to provide. By this example, we see how life can become a living prayer. When we become aware of the presence of God in every moment, we are taking part in a life of love. Offering one's daily duties to God obliges us to labor for the salvation of the souls whom He has entrusted to us. Each and every encounter, each and every person placed in our path is an opportunity for us to love Jesus.

Daily Prayer: Veni Creator, Ave Maris Stella

---

[18] Eymard, *Our Lady of the Blessed Sacrament*, 10-15.

The Immaculate Conception and Holy Communion

"Mary's Immaculate Conception was foretold in the terrestrial Paradise. The Most Holy Virgin is that blessed woman who was to crush with her heel the head of the infernal serpent. God in creating Mary immaculate, scores His great victory over the devil; He reestablishes His sovereignty over the earth, God reenters creation as Master. But behold Mary. God overshadows her. Mary is, by her purity, God's paradise with her, He will renew the world.[19] - St. Peter Julian

Through the Immaculate Conception, Mary was able to carry the mercy of God's Love into the world. We are consecrating our life to God by the way of our Lady of the Most Blessed Sacrament. Through this consecration we enter the same womb that carried the Son of God into the world, the womb of Mary. To become pure, we need to enter into this vessel of God's grace that was left immaculate so that we can be born of Mary. She will clothe us in the virtues of her Love.

"Blessed are the clean of heart, for they will see God" (Matthew 5:8). In the Eucharist we receive God's love, and in turn, we give that love by the sacrifices we make for our communities, families, and friends. The incarnate life of Jesus makes it possible to make every day a new beginning, to make every day a pure act of thanksgiving, to make every day a

---

[19] Ibid., p.16-21.

22

reciprocal act of love by our Adoration of the Blessed Sacrament. If you cannot get to daily Mass, offer a spiritual Communion. In the reception of Holy Communion, we come with the faith that longs to be pure of heart.

"Mary, teach us the life of Adoration." We come into a world in need of our baptismal life and promise of the Heavenly Father. We promise to live in God's grace. Mary is the gift God has given us to bring us closer to Him.

*Daily Prayer: **Veni Creator, Ave Maris Stella***

The Dowry of Mary Immaculate

On the day of her Immaculate Conception, Mary received a magnificent dowry in keeping with her sublime duties and her incomparable dignity as Mother of God. She received then that treasure of grace which was to make her the co-redemptrix of mankind, partner in the work of salvation. She never missed an opportunity of practicing virtue. She welcomed all the rays of God's holiness, absorbing them into her being without letting anything to be loss. She trembled before an angel. Mary never thought that she had done enough. Her later life was a prolonged martyrdom without the least alleviation. Mary embroidered the robe of her Immaculate Conception. It is only through our purity and holiness that we can prevail with God. God can only accomplish great things in pure souls. With what watchful care should we not guard our Baptismal innocence! If we have lost it we must purify it by penance. We must be pure. Without purity we can never please the Eucharistic God, for He is purity itself for purity is love.[20] – St. Peter Julian

St. Peter Julian Eymard's spiritual insight can move the deep recesses of the heart. How can we bring the message he is conveying into our lives? If Mary is the co-redemptrix of mankind, the partner in the work of salvation with Jesus, then our call is to ask for grace. Every time we say the Hail Mary, we ask her who is "-full of grace to pray for us sinners. It is a

[20] Ibid., 22-27.

very good practice to ask for grace daily. Grace will help us grow in virtue, grow in purity, grow in wisdom, and ultimately grow in love.

We think for a moment here, Mary trembled before an angel. Perhaps her trembling was from never thinking she did enough for the Almighty; her love was magnificent. Mary's later years of prolonged martyrdom reveal to us her knowledge of the merits of offering suffering up to receive back the gift of grace. This reality is what made her give to the Father with absolute purity. The anguish of her heart that she offered to God brought grace, for even after the Crucifixion Mary sacrificed for sinners. The jewels she placed on her robe were gifts offered in love to God. We too are invited to create a robe of salvation with our lives by the way of living out the Sacraments. Jesus living in the Eucharist is the greatest of all Sacraments of Grace available to us. Mary, teach us the life of Adoration!

Daily Prayer: *Veni Creator, Ave Maris Stella*

The Nativity of the Blessed Virgin

Let us rejoice in the birth of our Queen and Mother, which filled heaven with joy, earth with hope, and hell with terror. The Word willed to be born of a royal mother. Earthly pomp does not constitute royalty, that is only its outward show. However, the day was to come on which Mary's royalty, as that of her son, would be proclaimed and receive due honor. But before that day should come, He had to win it back by a life of humility, poverty, and suffering. Mary possessed all supernatural greatness. Supernatural greatness is but the reflection of God upon a creature whom He associates Himself in power and glory. The Father calls her His daughter, the Son loves her as His Mother, while the Holy Ghost guards her as His spouse. She was destined to share in the great work of divine power. Mary was born with all personal greatness. Even before birth she was penetrated with divine light, she had given herself to God completely. She loved Him. Oh! if we could have seen in spirit the birth of Mary, have seen this sun coming up out of the ocean of god's love. Never had any other creature such a birth. And the demons tremble; they behold her advancing against them, "strong as an army in battle array." Mary's birth heralds that of the Savior. Mary brings us the Bread of Life. From the day of her birth we salute her as the aurora of the Eucharist, for we know that the Savior of mankind will take from her the substance of that Body and Blood which He will give us in the Adorable Sacrament of His love.[21] – St. Peter Julian

First, we must remind ourselves of what we are doing. We are consciously taking up the daily reflections as a vow of our love to Jesus in the Blessed Sacrament, an offering at the end of this preparation time. This excerpt is yet another great entry into the consecration preparation, for we are to be born of Mary.

St. Peter Julian Eymard recalls her birth, the purity in which God needed to enter into the world. The Creator willed to show us through Mary the dignity of our lives. We are the daughters and sons of a King and Queen. St. Peter Julian continues with the words, "Mary's birth heralds that of the Savior."

St. John the Baptist is the usual one pointed to as herald: "Prepare the way of the Lord, make straight his paths" (Mark 1:3); " He must increase; I must decrease." (John 3:30). Mary is herald to the herald by bringing us the Promise of the Father. She brings us the Bread of Life.

Mary is often portrayed as the humblest of servants, the meekest, and the most gentle, but St. Peter Julian Eymard tells us she is as, "strong as an army in battle array."[22] God reflected all of His supernatural power and greatness through Mary's own crown of thorns. This excerpt calls to mind Mary's royal diadem. The crown of jewels was placed upon her in exchange for her crown of acceptance to the will of God. Mary held no denial, no resentment, and no withdrawal. She offered total consent to the incarnate life within her- God's Love made

---

[21] Ibid., 28-32.
[22] Ibid., (Note: phrase references Song of Songs).

manifest. The day of Eve was won back by Mary's true humility, poverty, and suffering. May we be born of Mary, coming forth from her womb into the world as heirs to the King, Jesus, by way of the Queen, Mary, Our Mother. Mary, teach us the life of Adoration.

Think of times that you have acted rather than trusted and waited in prayer for God to calm a storm in your life.

Daily Prayer: Veni Creator, Ave Maris Stella

Week 1 - Day 5

Mary's Presentation in the Temple

Mary had no childhood in the ordinary sense of the word. All her faculties were directed towards God, for He was her very life. Little Mary was always called to conciliate the disputants and impart to them that peace which she carried with her wherever she went. She lived a very simple life. She was the servant of all. It is her hidden life in the Temple that Mary should be our model. God had her even suspecting the great mission that she was to fulfill. Silence and seclusion are the soul of great things. So it is with us; if we wish to grow we must hide ourselves, we must remain unknown to the world, otherwise the demon will raise up many contradictions and the breath of self-love will destroy us. Our Lord has prepared us a long time. He has hedged us about with graces from our infancy, in order to introduce us into the cenacle of his Eucharist. He is in our midst; He is with us always. Let us imitate the silence, the solitude, the hidden life of our Blessed Mother. Let us, then, love the simple, hidden life, the obscure employments of our state in life; let us find our happiness in being unknown; let us hide the tiny flame of our lamp under a bushel, for the least breath of wind may extinguish it. Mary gave herself promptly, unreservedly, and forever. She gave Him her mind, her heart, her liberty--she kept nothing back. Oh, let us give all to Jesus Eucharistic, who gives Himself entirely to us. Let us rely on His grace and on our Mothers intercession, and when opportunity offers, let us recall her perfect oblation of herself to God. Her example will be our strength and encouragement.[23] – St. Peter Julian

We read the words left to us by St. Peter Julian Eymard and our hearts are elevated to the truth.

Day five continues by painting a picture of Mary's purity. Her life in God from a very early age manifests itself by taking the purity of her life of love into service. Mary's virtues and desire for reconciliation were an innate God-given quality that she acted upon by offering peace to all.

Whatever duties our life calls us to, no matter how mundane they seem to us, we offer them with a greater awareness that they are done in the presence of God. Mary, willing, unreservedly, and eternally can offer herself with ease by living in the Divine presence. Offering our day to the Lord first thing in the morning helps us to place ourselves in the presence of God. By offering our daily duties in the spirit of God's love we set ourselves before Him desiring His peace, striving to do His will. We present ourselves to God just like Mary was presented in the Temple; she held nothing back. "Oh, let us give all to Jesus Eucharistic, who gives Himself entirely to us."[24]

Pray for a strong desire to receive Holy Communion. It is there that the Divine presence will continue to fill us with great hope and longing for Heaven.

St. Peter Julian Eymard tells us to hide the tiny flame. This tiny flame offering symbolizes our confidence in the reality of God's life in us. When this acknowledgment is made we become like Mary; a great flame blazing for Jesus by which

---

[23] Ibid., 33-37.
[24] Ibid.

St. Peter Julian further refers to in many of his writings. We trust that God sees the humble offering of our lives in the hidden flames of love we give to Him. He is never outdone in His generosity. These deeds will glorify the Heavenly Father. His light will then shine through us before others. "Just so, your light must shine before others, that they may see your good deeds and glorify your heavenly Father" (Matt 5:16).

Mary, teach us the life of Adoration. The Promise of the Father awaits us.

Mary's desire was always to impart peace, pray to bring peace to a relationship or situation that may be awaiting the intercession of your prayer and service.

Daily Prayer: Veni Creator, Ave Maris Stella

The Annunciation

For Mary to have been chosen to cooperate in the work of the Incarnation of the Word-the grandest of all divine works. The world believes only too willingly that perfection is found in greatness. But the Angel seeks out a lowly virgin. He comes to Mary. So the angel comes to a virgin. God admits only pure souls to His friendship. He pardons the sinner, but He unites Himself only to purity. Mary alone is full of grace. He dwells in the purity of thy heart, O Mary. Mary is the aurora that separates light from darkness. Mary was troubled at the words of praise addressed to her. True virtue never recognizes itself. And Mary replies: "Behold the handmaid of the Lord! Be it done to me according to thy word!". She pleased the Lord by her virginity, she conceived Him by her humility. Silence and modesty are the safeguards of purity. This mystery of the Annunciation ennobles us for it brings God back to earth. It is, at the same time, a mystery entirely interior, a mystery of Communion. Jesus Eucharistic becomes, in a manner, incarnate in us, and Communion is the object of His Incarnation. By communicating worthily, we enter into the Divine plan, we complete it. Mary did not receive the Word for herself alone. She rejoiced that we should be able to participate in her happiness. Let us strive to imitate her virtues so that Jesus Christ may find in us, as in His holy Mother, a dwelling worthy of Him.[25] – St. Peter Julian

---

[25] Ibid., 38-44.

"Blessed are the pure in heart for they shall see God" (Matt 5:8). St. Peter Julian tells us that we should strive to imitate the virtues of Our Lady so that Jesus may find in us, as He did in His holy mother, a dwelling worthy of Him. We enter into God's divine plan by receiving the Eucharist. Following St. Peter Julian's thoughts, we unlock the message. We enter into Mary's maternal womb with humility, purity, and the reception of Holy Communion. Our free will brings us the same joy that Mary experienced in her fiat. We need to protect our choices with prayer, begging light from the Eucharist. Prudence is something that we should fight for by interceding with prayer before the Blessed Sacrament. We should ask what to do with the knowledge about the things that ought to be avoided. Prudence will keep us in the divine plan. Keep in mind the great connection of our bodies and souls. Fasting can help purify by keeping our senses mortified thus finding a way to better identify with God and others. Mortifying our senses to perfection will help purify our heart, mind, body and soul. Our Mother would want us to care for our bodies for they are temples of the Holy Spirit (fasting outside of the requirements of the Catechism should be guided by the direction of a priest). Our Lady's life in God was not for herself, it was a supernatural life of love that was to be given and continues to be given to us. Mary, Teach us the Life of Adoration. Pray and offer a sacrifice for the love of God this day.

Daily Prayer: Veni Creator, Ave Maris Stella

The First Adorer of the Incarnate Word

Behold my model, my mother, Mary, the first adorer of the Incarnate Word in her womb. In what did the perfection of Mary's adoration consist, at the first moment of the Incarnation? It was an adoration of humility, of self-annihilation before the sovereign majesty of God because, impelled by so much benevolence and love for her and all mankind, He had made choice of her, His humble handmaid, to be the mother of the Messiah. The second of Mary's acts of adoration would naturally be one of Joyous gratitude for God's ineffable and infinite goodness to man. Gratitude is an outpouring of the soul. The third act of the Blessed Virgin's adoration would have been an act of oblation, of self-sacrifice: the entire gift of herself, of her life, to the service of God. The last act of Mary's adoration was, doubtless, an act of tender compassion for poor sinners, for whose salvation the Word became Incarnate. She offered herself to do penance for them, in order to obtain their pardon and their return to God. She begged for them the happiness of knowing their Creator and their Redeemer; the grace of loving and serving Him, and thus rendering to the Most Holy Trinity the honor and glory which is Their due. O that I could adore our Lord as Mary did, for I possess Him, as she did, in Holy Communion. I desire henceforth to adore Thee in union with the Mother of adorers, the Queen of the Cenacle.[26] – St. Peter Julian

---

[26] Ibid., 45-48.

"He rested on the seventh day from all the work he had undertaken" (Gen 2:2). God can rest in us as we transform into His love. Transformation is the gift of formation. The Incarnation that continues through us promises infinite goodness to man. We are grateful to receive Jesus in Holy Communion. This is the greatest formation, a personal relationship with God who becomes incarnate in us. Transformation can only happen when we try to remain in God's Grace. Love is the real transformation. Like Mary, we will become joyous in our gratitude of God's life in us. St. Peter Julian Eymard tells us, "Gratitude is an outpouring of the soul."[27] The cenacle of our hearts becomes united to the cenacle of the upper room, where the Promise of the Father is fulfilled. God the Father is with us, and the Promise remains with us on the Altar of the Lord. Jesus directs and guides us in our union with Him. We need to remain connected to this promise: "I am the vine, you are the branches. Whoever remains in me and I in him will bear much fruit, because without me you can do nothing" (John 15:5). Like Mary, oblation and compassion will be the fruit of Jesus forming His life in our souls upon the reception of Holy Communion. The heart of God offers us reciprocity in our love for Him. Mary teaches us her way of returning love by praying for those who are so lost and hurt that they cannot even pray themselves. We lift up our hearts with her for them. This act makes us children of Mary, who keeps us in the mantle of her maternal love. Mary, teach us the life of Adoration. Think of ways to keep Sunday more Holy.

Daily Prayer: Veni Creator, Ave Maris Stella

---

[27] Ibid.

WEEK TWO

THEME: MOTHER OF GOD

Intention this week:

Make a perpetual promise to recite a spiritual communion prayer if you cannot get to daily Mass. The faith you place in the prayer is the grace you will receive from it. Continue to journal and prepare for a good and humble confession. Think of ways you can sacrifice in humble service to God. Offer something that will help you identify with another.

Prayers for each day this week (found in Appendix A)

- Veni Creator
- Litany of the Holy Spirit

Week 2 - Day 1

The Dignity of the Divine Maternity

Mary, Mother of Jesus the Son of God. Behold the sublime praise that the Gospel bestows on Mary! Because she was to be the mother of God she was given all sanctifying grace, all honor. When one calls her "Mother of God," one has said everything. Mary came to restore the human race, to restore to motherhood that crown of honor and nobility which Eve lost by her sin. Satan uncrowned our first mother: Mary reinstates her. Mary conceived God; she bore in her virginal womb, the Savior of the world, the source of love.

Behold the strong woman, "the Mother" par excellence. Crown of authority--this, then, is the second privilege of her Divine Maternity! There was also given to Mary a crown of glory. Mary gave birth to the Savior in joy. She knew not the pain of maternity. The Savior in passing through her womb bequeathed his glory, and Mary will be Queen because she has given to the world Jesus Christ, King. She is Queen of the angels, Queen of the Church. This is the honor, the dignity, and the glory of the Divine Maternity: Mary is honored, powerful and glorious in Jesus and by Jesus. She is His Divine Mother![28] – *St. Peter Julian*

St. Peter Julian Eymard states that one has said everything when one calls Mary, "Mother of God." Mary is Mother of the

---

[28] Ibid., 49-53.

Church, Mother of the Divine Maternity, Mother of the living Word of God, and Mother of Love. It may seem like a typical title for Week II, Mother of God. However, if we take the words of St. Peter Julian and proclaim them in awe, they will become what he said, everything. Mary is the Mother of God and our Mother. This is personal. This is our life in the Catholic Church. We are blessed to have a Mother. We are called within this upcoming week, Week II of this consecration preparation promise, to find ways to stay close to our Mother. This relationship must be nourished by our love as her children. We have the gifts, and we are called to use them. Otherwise, they will be passed on to others. St Peter Julian Eymard pleads with us to find the Eucharistic Jesus to conquer the concupiscence of sin. Jesus is our only hope. The Mother of God helps us find the Eucharistic Jesus.

All devotions should be helping us to find Divine charity. This is the end all that will be before us when we see the face of Jesus. Our Lady of the Blessed Sacrament will help us find the grace and wisdom of her Son. We pray to Jesus through Our Lady of the Blessed Sacrament's intercession. We immerse ourselves in the Holy Rosary as her children. We pray the life of Jesus Christ on these beads and then apply the virtues connected to all of the Sacred Mysteries to our own lives. We pray the scriptures when we pray the Most Holy Rosary.

Our consecration will move our hearts to make our Blessed Mother greater known and loved. This love for Mary can only point to the ultimate love, that of her Divine Son in the Blessed Sacrament. We are called to adorn her altars, to make special the great solemnities and feast days devoted to her. We are to unite in a unique fidelity as her consecrated children. We who are called to take a vow, this consecration vow, are called to love more in her name for the glory of the one whom we worship, Jesus Christ.

Proclaim the name, Mother of God. We offer these words in each Hail Mary, "Holy Mary, Mother of God, pray for us sinners." Every time we recite the Hail Holy Queen we say, "Pray for us O Holy Mother of God, that we may be made worthy of the promises of Christ, Amen."

The Promise of the Father has given us a great gift. We thank God by loving Mary and asking her how to love the Son of the Father. This is a small return for a priceless gift.

This week we keep the reflections alive in our heart by way of prayer. We honor this Mother of God as St. Peter Julian Eymard invites us to; "Honor your father and your mother, that you may have a long life in the land the LORD your God is giving you" (Exodus 20:12). We honor Jesus by praying to our Mother so that she may intercede for us.

These words are worth repeating from St. Peter Julian:

Mary gave birth to the Savior in joy. She knew not the pain of maternity. The Savior in passing through her womb bequeathed his glory, and Mary will be Queen because she has given to the world Jesus Christ, King. She is Queen of the angels, Queen of the Church.

Mary, Mother of God and our Mother, pray for us.

Daily Prayer: Veni Creator, Litany of the Holy Spirit

The Interior Life of Mary

Mary adorned with all gifts, enriched with all virtues, incomparable in merit, appeared to the world under a most ordinary exterior. Her life was passed in silence and obscurity, and the Gospel narrative says nothing about it. This was because Mary was supposed to be an illustrious model of the hidden life--a life hidden in God with Jesus Christ-a life which we should strive to honor and faithful copy in our conduct. I wish to show that the law of holiness which God follows in our souls, is the very same that He followed in Mary. The Eternal Father gave her all her virtues as Mother; the Son, all graces of Redemption; the Holy Ghost, the grace of love. Must we not, therefore, conclude that the retired, interior life is the most perfect? The exterior life, even when dedicated to God is less perfect. The Saints were formed on His Model. To be a friend of God, one must be ground to powder, reduced to nothing, annihilated as Jesus and Mary were.

Hence I say, if we wish to become saints, we must become interior souls. Without this interior spirit, how can we pray? If in the presence of our Lord we cannot spend a single instant without a book, if we have nothing to say to Him from our own heart, what are we going to do at Adoration? Let us strive to become recollected, interior souls. Without the interior life, we shall never receive any consolation, encouragement in prayer; we shall only be unhappy at the feet of our Lord. If we wish to become true adorers, we must have this interior spirit. But to discover the Heart of Jesus, we must be interior. He speaks to the recollected soul. He is wholly interior in the Blessed Sacrament. When the soul does not expand in His presence it is because He does not act upon it- there is some obstacle in His path. Oh, how I should wish to see accomplished in us what was so fully realized in the Blessed Virgin: "The kingdom of God is within you"-the kingdom of love, of virtue, and of all interior graces! In order to grow strong, to endure, we must descend to the very depths, even to self-annihilation. There we shall find Jesus. He is there annihilated. Oh, may that the Blessed Mother, our perfect exemplar of the interior life, make us live, as she did, in Jesus! May, we like her, remain always in him and never leave Him![29]- *St. Peter Julian*

Let us begin with a question. If someone asked you, "What is this consecration through Our Lady of the Blessed Sacrament?" Or better yet, if God asked you, "What is this consecration through Our Lady of the Blessed Sacrament?" Would your answer be, "Well, I have to accomplish the daily tasks of readings, my daily Marian prayers, litanies, and of course the Holy Rosary"? Although these are all necessary, they would not hold any merit to God without the gift of ourselves. The purity of our intentions offered in return for God's great love is an entrance into the answer. The interior life we are invited to, the hidden light given in humility, connects us to God. This humble service brings us to the correct response to God's question: "What does this consecration through Our Lady of the Blessed Sacrament mean to you?"

St. Peter Julian shares his very heart with us with the grace Mary led him to, which he expresses in these words, "But it

---

[29] Ibid., 54-58.

was through Mary that God made His will known to His servant." St. Peter Julian continues, "humbly submitting to the will of God."[30]

The handing over of our will to the Divine Will, so God's life may live through us, is our consecration promise to Jesus through Our Lady of the Blessed Sacrament. The answer is in the will, the continued fiat, the continued yes, the continued good that will be accomplished through us. Do not let anything stop you if you have chosen this devotion. Falling behind on the readings is of no importance if you have the intention to read when you can. This is a time to be with our Mother. She will always take us to the mercy of Jesus, lead us to the will of God, and direct us to the guidance of the Holy Spirit.

Yes, we strive to embrace all the devotions that raise our hearts and our minds to God. The greatest thereof is to try to find time to adore before the Eucharistic Lord, along with the practice of receiving Holy Communion daily or making a fervent spiritual Communion. Yet, the handing over of our will in humble submission, allowing God to live His life through us, is the continued conquering of original sin. We will always have in our human nature inclination to sin. Pride is hard to kill. Humility can begin with a simple choice. We can make a practice to turn all things to God, His goodness, and His life in us. With every simple choice placed before us we can try to choose through prayer what would be pleasing to Our Father. This is what Our Lady did. She immersed herself in the life of the Trinity. The life that was prepared for Her was no battle. Our Blessed Mother lived in the grace of God, in His peace, in His love, even amid the crosses, toils, and disappointments of

---

[30] Ibid., 57.

the sins of the world. Even standing at the foot of the Cross, her will was handed over to God. St. Peter Julian tells us one has said everything when one calls Mary the Mother of God. She looks for nothing, yet we can in loving return say, "Yes Mary, you are deserving of this title. We have recourse to thee. We love thee. Guide us to the will of the Father."

Daily Prayer: Veni Creator, Litany of the Holy Spirit

Modesty, a Characteristic of Mary's Life

Mary's hidden life possesses a characteristic that distinguishes it from that of Jesus. Mary's life is always the same, simple and hidden, profoundly humble and modest. Modesty was a characteristic of her piety, of her virtues, and of all her actions. Mary was modest in her exterior. We too should try to avoid attracting attention to ourselves, by the modesty of behavior, if we wish to resemble our Blessed mother in her life.

Mary was modest in the world. She spoke no word in her own praise, nor did she bring forward her title Mother of God, nor the power and glory of her Son in order to gain the esteem of men. Mary was modest in her duties. She fulfilled them with sweetness, without eagerness, always satisfied, always prepared to take up some new duty. She is, therefore, a beautiful model for all those who wish to live the life of Jesus Eucharistic. The life of an adorer, consecrated to the service of the Eucharistic King, is composed of little sacrifices which God alone sees and rewards. The lowliness of his service constitutes all the honor, all the joy of his filial devotedness, and his sole ambition is to please his Master by the constant sacrifice of self. Mary was modest in her piety. Mary elevated to the highest degree of prayer to which any creature can attain, lived in the habitual exercise of perfect love, exalted about all the Angels, and by her dignity of Mother of God an order apart in the wonders of God. Her humility saw only the goodness of God. Behold the great secret of perfection: to know how to find it in what is most simple; to know how to nourish it in what is most common. Let us love the little virtues of Nazareth, those hidden virtues that are born at the foot of the Cross, under the shadow of Jesus and Mary; then shall we fear neither the tempest that shatters the cedars nor the thunderbolt that strikes the mountain top.

Mary was modest in her sacrifices. She was modest in enduring the anguish of her holy spouse. (She) waited for Heaven to vindicate her virtue, calmly abandoning herself to Divine Providence. With her heart pierced with sorrow, Mary followed her Son bearing His Cross; plunged in an immeasurable sorrow, sorrow as deep as her love, Mary suffered in silence. Finally, Mary was modest in her glory, and this is the most wonderful triumph of Mary's modesty. Mary by reason of her remarkable dignity as Mother of God has the right to the homage of the universe, yet Mary retained only that anguish and the sacrifice of her motherhood. If then, we desire to be true children of this loving Mother, we must clothe ourselves with her modesty. Let her modesty be the rule of our conduct.

Modesty is the sovereign virtue of an adorer since it is the virtue of the servants of kings, and the virtue of the Angels in the Divine Majesty. We must be modest even as Mary, in the service of Jesus.[31] *– St. Peter Julian*

We are the children of the Mother of God, this modest mother, who carried the Son of God into the world. This existence of God's life will continue to be transferred through the love of Mary's children- through the incarnation of her Son living in us. We are marked by our Baptism as adopted children of God. The promise of the Father has been kept through Our Holy Redeemer, Jesus Christ, and given to us by

[31] Ibid., 59-65.

47

Mary. We have a responsibility to be heirs of the King, to bear witness to the love of God, "and the servant who was ignorant of his master's will but acted in a way deserving of a severe beating shall be beaten only lightly. Much will be required of the person entrusted with much, and still more will be demanded of the person entrusted with more" (Luke 12:48).

We who are consecrated must carry the love of God into the world. We may not be scholars, theorists, or theologists, but we can, by our own relationship with the Heavenly Father, learn to give of ourselves. Mary's modesty clothed her entire existence into the comfort of our creator. She had full confidence in the love of God. Mary's tears continue to fall from the beatific vision for all that is lost. Her tears fall in modesty and in the hope that we who love her will fight for those who, without Jesus, live in the incurable wound of original sin. We fight through the continued life of modesty, the hidden life of prayer, and the offering of our wills to God. We have been given much. We have much love to return in modesty to Jesus through the Mother of God. The fidelity of our love is part of the trustworthiness that is scarce to be found in our day. St. Peter Julian said, "Mary by reason of her remarkable dignity as Mother of God has the right to the homage of the universe, yet Mary retained only that anguish and the sacrifice of her motherhood."[32] We are called to mother the world, to sacrifice for the lost and lonely, to pray for those who persecute us. May we be Mary's reliable children to bear the responsibility of the souls of our brothers and sisters.

"The life of an adorer, consecrated to the service of the Eucharistic King, is composed of little sacrifices which God

---

[32] Ibid.

alone sees and rewards. The lowliness of his service constitutes all the honor, all the joy of his filial devotedness, and his sole ambition is to please his Master by the constant sacrifice of self."[33]

This consecration preparation should be taking us somewhere, or rather closer to someone, Jesus. Let the Mother of God take us to her Divine Son in modest submission to God's will for our lives.

Daily Prayer: Veni Creator, Litany of the Holy Spirit

---

[33] Ibid.

Week 2 - Day 4

Mary at Bethlehem

The mystery of Bethlehem is full of love and sweetness. Let us enter into the attitude of the mind of the Most Blessed Virgin. Let us unite with Mary in her expectation, during the hours that preceded the blessed moment of her Son's birth.

Mary knew from the Prophecies all the suffering that awaited her Son, and she was ready to serve Him in His way and to follow Him everywhere. Let us imitate this spirit of self-sacrifice, this true love.

St. Joseph's sorrow must indeed have been very great. It was incumbent on him as head of the family to find shelter for his holy spouse, and we can well imagine what must have been his anxiety, his distress, when, denied admittance everywhere, he was forced to lead Mary, about to bring for her the Child. Mary was happy even in the midst of these rebuffs. Man is disturbed; he seeks human helps, and when he has exhausted all known means in vain, God leads him where He wills. It is in this state of abandonment that we feel most sensibly the goodness of God. The Israelites received more favors in the desert than in the Promised Land; God was nearer to them there.

Who indeed could be more beautiful than Mary, even exteriorly? She is that pure lily of the valley that has grown in an immaculate soil. Mary is the paradise of God! ...Let us now penetrate into Mary's soul and contemplate its beauty. There is beauty enough there to give us unending happiness when we come to know it well. She becomes the ostensorium of the Word

Incarnate. She is the channel by which Jesus comes to us! The Eucharist began at Bethlehem in Mary's arms. It was she who brought to humanity the Bread for which it was famishing, and which alone can nourish it. She accepts God's will, and, bearing Him in her arms, herself prepares for us the Victim of Calvary- that Victim of our Altars. Some days later it is the Magi who bring their tribute of adoration and their royal gifts. Mary offers her Babe to their love: it is in her arms that they find Him.

To find Jesus in the arms of His Mother, to unite oneself to Mary's sentiments as she presses Him to her heart- O what a ravishing moment! Oh, wonderful moment in which all else is forgotten, in which we no longer desire anything else, not even heaven -for we possess it already, we have Jesus and Mary.[34] – *St. Peter Julian*

St. Peter Julian reminds us that, "we no longer desire anything else, not even heaven-for we possess it already, we have Jesus and Mary."[35] The consolation of every soul can be found in these words which direct us to the heart of the Eucharist. Our Lady of the Blessed Sacrament can only bring us to Jesus Eucharistic. The poverty of our spirit will be nourished by this divine reality. "Blessed are the poor in spirit, for theirs is the kingdom of Heaven" (Matthew 5:3). The Kingdom of Heaven is already found in the poverty of our spirit. We long for freedom, the true liberty that comes from being born of Mary. Jesus was born in poverty. We too must be born into the poverty of the Father's love, the poverty of our obedience to the will of God in our lives. We, like the Magi,

---

[34] Ibid., 66-71.
[35] Ibid.

pay homage by acceptance to God's will, His love, and life in us. St. Joseph was helpless; his poverty led him to hope in the help of the Heavenly Father.

The consecration promise we are entering into should permeate our existence. We no longer have to be on our own. We have our Mother. Mary will take us by the hand each day as a guide to the life of the Holy Spirit. The Holy Spirit of God's love made manifest by the life of Christ truly present in the Blessed Sacrament will set us free. God's mercy is new every morning; "They are new every morning, great is thy faithfulness" (Lamentations 3:23).

In our human existence, we will forever be in battle with the enemy of our salvation. "For our wrestling is not against flesh and blood; but against principalities and powers, against the rulers of the world of this darkness, against the spirits of wickedness in the high places" (Ephesians 6:12). How can we live in this world without a Mother? It is impossible. God would not have it so. A Mother prays, protects, and preserves life. We have a place to rest our head in this world like St. John at the last supper, on the heart of Jesus. Mary, as the good mother, ensures the place of rest for us. She is with us at every Holy Mass. She accompanies us as we receive Holy Communion into our very souls to embrace the life of Jesus, so we may love through this earthly journey. We live in the Paschal Mystery of our salvation through Holy Communion. In the simplicity of our humanity, all we need is to follow a daily practice. Rise and reach out to the Mother of God saying, "Good morning Mom, bring me to your Son!"

"Then you will know the truth, and the truth will set you free" (John 8:32).

"To find Jesus in the arms of His Mother, to unite oneself to Mary's sentiments as she presses Him to her heart- O what a ravishing moment! Oh, wonderful moment in which all else is forgotten, in which we no longer desire anything else, not even heaven -for we possess it already, we have Jesus and Mary."[36]

The Kingdom of Heaven is with us here at the Altar of the Lord, Jesus truly present in the Blessed Sacrament! Mary! Mother of God and our Mother pray for us.

Daily Prayer: Veni Creator, Litany of the Holy Spirit

---

[36] Ibid.

Jesus Presented in the Temple by Mary

Our Lord did not wish to delay his offering of Himself publicly to His Father. He inspires Mary to take Him to the Temple.

The joy, the bliss of the Most Blessed Virgin Mary came to an end that day. "And thy own soul a sword shall pierce." How can the Holy Trinity, how can God, so good, so tender, thus reveal such a mystery of sorrow to this poor young mother? Calvary is wherever Jesus is; everywhere does she behold Jesus crucified. When our soul is not strong in virtue, God lets us live a more or less shielded life: but when He sees a really loving soul, He hastens to crucify it in order to show forth His glory therein. Love entails suffering.

"He that does not take up his cross daily and follow Me is not worthy of Me."

We must not, of course disdain God's consolations, we must receive them joyfully when He sends them; but we must not seek them alone. It is by suffering that we are sanctified, by crosses and trials that the soul is strengthened, freed from self, in order that it may find its satisfaction in God, and God alone.

This is the lesson of the mystery of Mary's purification, and of Jesus' Presentation in the Temple. Let us put it into practice if we wish to be worthy of the August Victim, whom we incessantly contemplate in the Blessed Sacrament, and of His

Mother who so generously offered Him for us.[37] – *St. Peter Julian*

The Agony in the Garden is where Our Precious Lord sweat blood from the anguish of His heart. "Father, if you are willing, take this cup away from me; still, not my will but yours be done" (Luke 22:42). God offers us the mystery of our salvation by complete trust in Him. St. Peter Julian tells us, "Love entails suffering."[38] If love encompasses suffering, then we can only hope in finding this call for suffering through the One that loved us to the end, Jesus! "And from Jesus Christ, the faithful witness, the firstborn of the dead and ruler of the kings of the earth. To him who loves us and has freed us from our sins by his blood " (Revelation 1:5).

Mother of God teach us to pray. Whether this is a first-time consecration preparation or a renewal, the process should be taking us somewhere. Try to formulate a prayer routine and a method of praying that will raise your heart and mind to God. Since this devotion is dedicated to Our Lady of the Blessed Sacrament, it would be recommended to set some time aside for Jesus in the Eucharist. Try to uphold a schedule, yet always be open to what the day may have you busy doing without impressing guilt upon yourself. Spending some quiet time when you rise, uniting with the Heavenly Father, will offer peace for the day. Meditating on the mysteries of the Holy Rosary and the virtues connected with them will keep us close to Mary, who will always bring us to Jesus. We may memorize the daily consecration prayers if recited enough. Then the prayers will become etched in our hearts, penetrate our

---

[37] Ibid., 82-86.
[38] Ibid.

existence, and become part of us. If we fail to pray for a day, we will feel something missing and strive to achieve evermore the daily prayer routine.

Jesus awaits us in the Blessed Sacrament. It is there where we learn how to love. If love entails suffering, we need this relationship of love to prepare us for Calvary. We need to pray as Jesus did in the Garden. Without this connection to God, it will be impossible for us to give rise to the embrace of suffering. Mary, Mother of God and our Mother, bring us to the Eucharist where we find the Son of God.

We can believe in Jesus in His True Presence, and we can recognize Jesus in His True Presence, but when we enter into the love of Christ in His humanity we enter into a divine relationship. Jesus remains in humble service to us in this Bread of Life. By spending time with Jesus, He teaches us the love that will entail the sufferings of this present life. Jesus teach us to love through the Sacramental life you give us. Teach us to pray as you prayed. Teach us to go through Mary, Mother of God and our Mother.

Daily Prayer: Veni Creator, Litany of the Holy Spirit

Week 2 - Day 6

The Life of the Holy Family

Let us meditate upon the life of the Holy Family, the life of Mary and of Joseph in Jesus. Jesus was the center of Mary's and Joseph's love. "Where thy treasure is, there is thy heart." In the same way, my house, my family, my center is the Eucharist, the Tabernacle near which I dwell. Like Mary and Joseph should feel at home only there. Jesus was the end of Mary's and Joseph's existence; they lived only for Him; they labored for Him alone. And for us, too, Jesus Eucharistic should be the Object of our life, our joy- the inspiration of our work. What life could be more beautiful than that which is passed in the company of Jesus in the Most Blessed Sacrament! Jesus was the constant nourishment of Mary's and Joseph's life of union and love.

They beheld Him incessantly seeking after and selecting, by preference, occasions of poverty, obedience and penance. They contemplated his humility and self-annihilation, while they admired His fidelity in referring all to the glory of His father, never desiring, like mankind, to be the object of any praise, and glory. Jesus, Mary and Joseph had but one aim in life, they wished but for one thing, the honor and glory of the Heavenly Father.

This should be my ambition; but in order to accomplish this, I must unite myself with Mary and Jesus. I must share their life, their family life, that intimate life of which God alone holds the secret. O how happy is the soul in contemplating the hidden life of the Holy Family, all that is said and done therein-the Gospel of the family of Jesus! He reveals Calvary to them, tells them of all the humiliation and suffering which He has to pass. He shows them in His hands the places where the nails are to be driven; and this in order that Calvary may even now begin to bear fruit in the soul of His Mother and His holy guardian. He speaks to them of the church, of the Apostles, of the Religious Orders which will consecrate themselves to his and to their, honor. He speaks to them of us, our miseries, and of the immense love that He bears us. Nazareth has become a heaven of love, the paradise of the second Adam and the new Eve; a heaven of the purest virtues, of the holiest love. What a delicious perfume ascended to the Lord from that delectable garden in which blossomed the Incarnate Word, Mary, and Joseph the Just! The Heavenly Father found therein His delight; the angelic spirits looked upon it in admiration. As for me, I desire to gleam from it love for a pious and recollected life in Jesus, Mary and Joseph.[39] *– St. Peter Julian*

We are, believe it or not, entering the halfway point of our consecration preparation to Jesus through Our Lady of the Blessed Sacrament. Our first consecration promise should be our dedication to the Liturgy, the reception of Holy Communion and the living Word of God. This devotion to consecrate oneself to the specific title of Our Lady should incessantly expand our desire to be born of Mary into the incarnate life of God. We embody the life of Jesus in our very own being when we receive Him in a state of grace. This should inspire a longing in our hearts to serve, like St. Peter Julian recommends to us,

---

[39] Ibid., 78-82.

He (Jesus) reveals Calvary to them, (Mary and Joseph) tells them of all the humiliation and suffering through which He has to pass. He shows them in His hands the places where the nails are to be driven; and this in order that Calvary may even now begin to bear fruit in the soul of His Mother and His holy guardian. He speaks to them of the church, of the Apostles, of the Religious Orders which will consecrate themselves to His and to their, honor. He speaks to them of us, our miseries, and of the immense love that He bears us.[40]

What return of love can we possibly offer in the short time we have upon this earth to God? The penances we give reclaim what we have lost by sin. Those who give back must be the chosen ones who have said yes in hope of the resurrection. " It was not you who chose me, but I who chose you and appointed you to go and bear fruit that will remain, so that whatever you ask the Father in my name he may give you" (John 15:16). Mary's faithful children will allow the Holy Spirit to inspire a return for the love that has been poured out. We can place many rules upon ourselves, even in our spiritual lives, as an offering. If we pray for the union of divine love when we are before Jesus in the Blessed Sacrament, the call to give will flow like a natural response from the Father's love for us. The fear of the Lord will be upon us. We will love more and more and be less inclined to hurt Our Father who loves us so much.

Pray for the grace to choose the heavier crosses, to choose the things that would be less attractive to us and more pleasing

---

[40] Ibid.

to God. These are simple ways to find love. We need not go very far. We can all soul search to see things right before us that may make a difference in the life of another.

St. Joseph and St. John, two men of divine grace, were given to Mary, and she offers them back to us as intercessors of immense love, fidelity, and heritage. The Holy Family was modeled to us by St. Joseph. The new covenant of God's love, offered to us without end at the last supper, was recognized first by St. John, the Beloved Disciple. St. Joseph's life of divine union with the Heavenly Father and St. John's martyred love of the Holy Eucharist continue to guide us to the Heart of Christ Jesus.

Daily Prayer: Veni Creator, Litany of the Holy Spirit

Week 2 - Day 7

Mary's Compassion

Mary had neither original nor actual sin to expiate. How was it, then, that she, the sinless one, should have to suffer so much all her life? Suffering is the law of love; it was Mary's love that made her martyrdom, and because she loved more than any other creature, she suffered an incomparable martyrdom. Suffering is the actual glorification of Jesus Christ in us. By suffering, we continue and complete His Sacrifice.

Maternity is purchased by suffering. Let us, then, reflect upon Mary's participation in the Passion of Jesus, and try to understand the part she took in it.

By a supernatural light, Mary saw Jesus in the Garden of Olives; she shared in His prayer, His sorrow, His agony, for there was perfect love and sympathy between those two hearts. Later she saw Jesus betrayed by Judas, abandoned by all, denied by Peter. She arrives at the praetorium: she hears the stokes of the scourging.

She follows Him to Calvary.

What a sight for a mother! She too is being crucified- the rebounds of the hammer give Mary her stigmata. She hears Jesus cry out that He has been forsaken by His Heavenly Father! -her well-beloved Son has breathed His last sigh. What does Mary do now? She is in the agony of grief and love, Mary's life will now be passed in recalling the sorrows of the Passion, in order to renew her own martyrdom and the glory rendered to God by her sufferings. She will retrace again and again that

*path of sorrow, and so be the first to teach us the pious devotion-
so powerful with Jesus, and so useful to the soul- The way of the
Cross.[41] – St. Peter Julian*

Eucharistic adorers will identify with the suffering
members of the Mystical Body of Christ. It is a grace that will
come to those who spend time with Jesus in the Blessed
Sacrament. Mary will teach us this law of love that she knew
too well. Mary was one with Jesus. St. Peter Julian states so
perfectly, "for there was perfect love and sympathy between
those two hearts."[42] Mary suffered in the Paschal Mystery as if
it were herself enduring the pain. She was there with a total
embrace of the torture that her Son endured. She probably
would have been less pained if it were her that experienced all
the agony. Mary's love is a model for us; she is the one to show
us the way of the Cross. Jesus Himself met her on His way. We
too must meet her. This relationship is a divine gift from God.

As consecrated children, we live in the Paschal Mystery,
the Passion, Death, and Resurrection of Christ. Those who are
suffering become our suffering, " If [one] part suffers, all the
parts suffer with it; if one part is honored, all the parts share its
joy" (1Corinthians 12:26). St. Peter Julian continues, "suffering
is the actual glorification of Jesus Christ in us. By suffering, we
continue and complete His Sacrifice."[43] Our lives continue to
become a living prayer when we live out the Holy Sacrifice of
the Mass in our lives. We become more like the One who we
receive and offer His life to all. The sacrifices come from the
depths of our love for Jesus Christ. Like Mary, we want to give

---

[41] Ibid., 83-87.
[42] Ibid.
[43] Ibid.

back for all of the blessings. Our Blessed Mother's heart of love came from love, the love of Jesus. She witnessed this love, adored this love, embraced this love, and became this love.

True joy can only come from the truth of God's revealed life in us. The crosses we embrace offered back with a grateful heart will give praise to the Heavenly Father. The mystery of our salvation is recognized by our longing to serve. It is in the act of giving that our consciences are formed in God. Mary was graced with the light of Heaven, unveiled to her by the union of her heart to the will of the Promise of the Father. Her complete trust empowered by the Holy Spirit offered her the grace to withstand Calvary and the passion that led to it. Mary, teach us the law of love, teach us to sacrifice for one another. Teach us to identify with the pains and sorrows of others as if they were our own. Teach us to offer up all that is displeasing to us in the spirit of joy for the love of Our Heavenly Father. Mary, Mother of God, pray for us.

Daily Prayer: Veni Creator, Litany of the Holy Spirit

WEEK THREE

THEME: MARY, TEACH US THE LAW OF LOVE

Intention this week:

Make a perpetual promise to recite a spiritual communion prayer if you cannot get to daily Mass. The faith you place in the prayer is the grace you will receive from it. Continue to journal and prepare for a good and humble confession. Try to find time to spend with Jesus in the Blessed Sacrament. Pray for the gift to make an act of charity for someone.

Prayers for each day this week (found in Appendix A)

- Veni Creator
- Our Lady of the Blessed Sacrament

Mary After the Resurrection

As Mary had suffered in union with her Son dying upon the Cross, so did she share in His joy and happiness after His Resurrection; the life of Mary always conformed to the life of Jesus and faithfully reflected it. He parted from her in tears, he returns to her with joy! What a moment for Mary, when her Risen Jesus embraces her with all the love and respect that she merited!

Only through love's insight can we reconstruct that scene. Spiritual vision is always proportionate to the soul's sanctity. But our Lord did not come to visit Mary alone: He was accompanied by retinue of all those Saints who had risen with Him. And St. Joseph, St. Joachim and St. Ann, did they not also come to pay their visit of respect and love? The sight of the Blessed Virgin must indeed have filled the Saints with joy, so pure a reflex of Jesus' light.

So our Lord leaves His Mother not only consoled, but in an ecstasy of bliss when he goes to show Himself to Mary Magdalen and His Apostles. After having given Jesus to the world, Mary was bound to be eclipsed; she had to remain in the background in order to become the model of interior souls, the patroness of the lowly, hidden life. Mary's mission after her Son's Resurrection was one of love and prayer. Our Lord seems to have kept for Himself alone the secret of his Mother's life; He wished it to be entirely for Himself.

Mary devoted herself to guard Him in the privacy of a life entirely devoted to prayer. Had Mary not consecrated herself to this state, we adorers of the Eucharist could never have found in her our model. But Mary, the unknown servant, and custodian of the Holy Eucharist is our Mother and her life is our grace.

The Resurrection of her Son produced in Mary this prodigy: it absorbed her life, transformed it into the Risen Life of Jesus- a life wholly interior, invisible, separated from all created things and uninterruptedly united with God. Let us remember the more interior the life, the more perfect it is. But it is the lot of souls who, like Mary, desire to love only our Lord and to be known only to Him.[44] – St. Peter Julian

Mary, teach us the law of love, "I tell you, unless your righteousness surpasses that of the scribes and Pharisees, you will not enter into the kingdom of heaven" (Matthew 5:20). Our charity must surpass that of the scribes and Pharisees. Mary had to become one with love to be love. The hidden life of love that she lived in union with the Heavenly Father elevated her soul to the resurrected life even while she remained on earth. Mary's charity was divine and could only come from her self-annihilation. St. Peter Julian states that "spiritual vision is always proportionate to the soul's sanctity."[45] Mary, conceived without sin, was in a constant state of grace. Her spiritual vision was as clear as day. The sanctity of her life was lived out on earth in perfect union with Heaven.

Mary's children live on the front line of God's love. We are called to forgive more, love more, and understand more the

---

[44] Ibid., 88-93.
[45] Ibid.

wisdom of Our Father. We fail, we fall, we hurt, we long for righteousness. We can only try to purify ourselves from sin and soul search deeply for how we can become more pleasing to God. The Sacrament of Penance should be a companion for us; the mercy of God waits for us there. St. Paul reminds us that he cannot even judge himself, "Who confers distinction upon you? What do you possess that you have not received? But if you have received it, why are you boasting as if you did not receive it?" (1 Corinthians 4:31). Judgement is a great battle for our souls. We must try to submit to the law of God's love. This is the law of love that Mary knew. She judged no-one, not even those who crucified her Son. Mary is the perfect example of divine charity, goodness, humility, and meekness. Mary is the perfect adorer of Jesus Eucharistic. St. Peter Julian tells us: "The Resurrection of her Son produced in Mary this prodigy: it absorbed her life, transformed it into the Risen Life of Jesus- a life wholly interior, invisible, separated from all created things and uninterruptedly united with God."[46] Perfect!

No exterior mode can see the interior of one's soul. The hidden life you live with God is the first tool for survival in the spiritual life. The Sacraments are our gifts. The Eucharist can never be desired too much. We adore Him, we love Him, we seek Him, until the end of time. We have the opportunity to receive Him, even daily. "Give us today our daily bread" (Matthew 6:11). God is with us. Mary knew this divine reality. She lived her life in the grace of God. St. Peter Julian says her life is our grace. Jesus is that grace, and He was, and for all eternity will be her life. Our Mother would only want to give her children everything; her grace is her Son. Mary longs to

---

[46] Ibid.

bring us ever closer to Jesus in the Blessed Sacrament. It is there we build Eucharistic communities, and a strong union of love that extends through the heart of Mary's children throughout the earth. Mary, teach us the law of love.

Daily Prayer: Veni Creator, Our Lady of the Blessed Sacrament

Week 3 - Day 2

Mary, Our Mother in the Cenacle

It is to our best interest to honor with a particular devotion the life of Mary in the Cenacle, altogether given up to the service and glory of the Eucharist. We must try to catch something of her spirit and love, in order to render our Divine Savior present in our midst, a worship of adoration more pleasing and more perfect, in union with that which His most holy Mother offered Him. To become good servants we must be docile and devout children of Mary. We take His place in Mary's heart. That good Mother loves us henceforth as her true children. She is the only true and perfect copy of His virtues. She knows all the secrets of the love of the Savior for mankind; she shares His unbounded love for us.

Our Lady's mission is to form Jesus in us. Mary would have died with Jesus at the foot of the Cross, "By my sacrifice I became the Savior and the Father of the great human family; but these poor children must have a mother. Do thou be their Mother, O thou strong one. Love them even as thou hast loved Me, as I have loved them. It was through love for them that I became Man, through love for them that My Heavenly Father made thee My Mother. It is for them that I am giving my blood and My life. I love them more than Myself, and I transfer to them all the claims that I have to thy maternal love. Whatever thou dost for them, will be done for Me. I confide to thee the fruits of My Redemption, the salvation of mankind, the care of My Church, the service of My Sacrament of Love. Form for Me true adorers in spirit and in truth, that they may adore Me as thou hast adored Me; that they may love Me as thou hast loved Me!"

This was Jesus' last legacy, signed with His Blood and ratified by the heart of Mary, His Blessed Mother. She had ascended Calvary with Jesus, to die with Him; she came down therefrom with the beloved disciple, her adopted son, with the holy women, her daughters. Later she would conduct them to the Eucharistic Cenacle, there to begin her Christian maternity at the foot of the Divine Sacrament.

It is she who will form a guard of honor for Jesus in the Eucharist; she it is who will train His servants.

Oh! Thank well this good Mother! You owe all the graces of your life to her, and the greatest of them all is that of loving and serving by the consecration of your entire life to Him, the King of kings on His Throne of Love.[47]-St. Peter Julian

"Do thou be their Mother, O thou strong one."[48] It may be a difficult task to get through St. Peter Julian Eymard's words without being brought to tears of joy by the reality of what God has given us in Mary, mother and strong one. We need not journey alone, not when we are offered the womb of Mary. She is forming us in her womb, birthing us into the Eucharistic Kingdom of God's Love, and nurturing us as mother of the human family. What consolation! What a gift from God! We who take this blessing seriously are called to keep it sacred. We keep it sacred by the faith we have in the promise of God's love. The crosses, toils, and disappointments of life will weigh

---

[47] Ibid., 94-97.
[48] Ibid.

us down. The enemy of our souls will place discouragements before us. We hope in Mary. We run to Mother. She is the Mother of Perpetual Help. Our Savior ran fast to her, losing His own sandal.[49] We too must run fast into the loving embrace of Mary to be taught this law of love. Mary, God's strong one!

The law of love is found in the presence of Jesus. We are brought to Him by our mother. Placed before the Blessed Sacrament, we find the One who serves, the One who loves, and the One who manifested the Promise of our Heavenly Father. The promise is to be found in humble service to God's Will for our lives. How our pride tries to take hold of life even in striving for the good. We fear, we try to overtake, trying to take control of what God is already in control of. We will find much peace in the trust we offer to God's plan for our eternal salvation. The Eucharistic Lord Jesus lovingly remains in this bread of life to teach us the way of peace. "Peace- I leave with you; my peace I give to you. Not as the world gives do I give it to you. Do not let your hearts be troubled or afraid" (John 14:27). In the silence we find the peace that our souls long for through the power of the Eucharist; our troubled hearts become not afraid.

"It is she who will form a guard of honor for Jesus in the Eucharist; it is she who will train His servants."[50] St. Peter Julian Eymard was proclaimed to be the Apostle of the Eucharist. His love for our Blessed Mother was rewarded with

---

[49]Since 1866 the Redemptorists have spread devotion to the Blessed Virgin Mary under the icon and title of Our Mother of Perpetual Help (also known as Our Lady of Perpetual Help). In the icon we see that, "in His hurry to reach his mother, Jesus has almost lost one of his sandals." https://redemptorists.net/redemptorists/devotion-to-omph/. (3/5/1019).
[50] Eymard, *Our Lady of the Blessed Sacrament*, 96.

the title, Our Lady of the Blessed Sacrament, which we celebrate every May 13th. Our Lady entrusted St. Peter Julian as the guard of the Eucharistic family. St. Peter Julian allowed God to take hold of his life. His gift of self was poured out from the very tears of his self-annihilation. He let go of himself to allow God's life to work through him. The Congregation of the Blessed Sacrament upholds the dignity lived through their patron St. Peter Julian Eymard. The service he labored was not in vain; it is the Eymardian Eucharistic family of God's love. His order beats with the Heart of Jesus Christ to make known the reality of Jesus truly present in the Blessed Sacrament. We are not alone. God would not have it so. The Son of Man remains with us and, with Mary by His side, gives us strength by His grace. We continue to be cared for. All we need to do is ask Mary to continue to teach us this law of Love. We find Him in the Blessed Sacrament. We recognize Him. We ask Him to teach us to love. Mary, teach us the law of love.

Daily Prayer: Veni Creator, Our Lady of the Blessed Sacrament

Week 3 - Day 3

Mary, Our Mistress in the Cenacle

"Disciple, behold thy Mother!" When Mary heard these words form the lips of her dying Son, words which mean so much to us, her soul suffered inexpressible anguish. What! the disciple instead of the Master; John instead of Jesus; the creature instead of the Son of God! But Our Blessed Mother lovingly accepts the substitution. Mary's mission will be to superintend our Christian education. Mary will have but to draw there from, to distribute the Bread that He left us.

She will conceive, will form and perfect Jesus in us. Her mission to which she is ever faithful, is to give us Jesus.

Happy is he who has received from her his first lessons in holiness;

Thus it is Mary who forms and guards, she makes piety sweet and easy. Sanctity that is fashioned by Jesus alone has an austere character; that which Jesus and Mary form together is more attractive. Let Mary then lead us to Jesus; let her teach us to know and to love Him. In this alone consists true sanctity and perfect happiness.[51]- St. Peter Julian

"Sanctity that is fashioned by Jesus alone has an austere character; that which Jesus and Mary form together is more attractive."[52] St. Peter Julian Eymard continues to bring light to the life-giving stream of God's love through the heart of Our

---

[51] Ibid., 98-103.
[52] Ibid.

Blessed Mother. He calls Mary our mistress, she who will supervise us into the Eucharistic Kingdom. We are her servants without question. Mary molds us into the profession of our faith. We become one, holy, catholic, and apostolic Church, entering into the tradition that our mother passes on to her children. This tradition we carry through the womb of Mary is the bread that comes down from Heaven. "I am the living bread that came down from heaven; whoever eats this bread will live forever; and the bread that I will give is my flesh for the life of the world" (John 6:51). Mary forms guards for her Son, who will find happiness and sanctity that flow from the Altar of the Lord.

Mary will conceive us into the perfection of Jesus throughout our lives. She accepts us at the foot of the cross in exchange for her Son. Mary takes hold of us for the love of Jesus. His life for our sins and her love for his life. We are blessed with a Mother.

"Can a mother forget her infant, be without tenderness for the child of her womb? Even should she forget, I will never forget you" (Isaiah 49:15). The Promise of the Father lives through the words, "I will never forget you." God will never abandon us. He completes His human family with the care of our Mother. Mary is the Mistress of the Cenacle. The cenacles of our hearts are formed by her, formed at every celebration of the Eucharist when we enter into the Mass by our participation. We offer ourselves in the likeness of our mother to our Heavenly Father. We pray for Mary's intentions united to our own. We become like our beneficent mother when we allow her to teach us the law of love. We are conceived into God's Eternal Love, in the Blessed Sacrament, and we bring it with us to Heaven by the guidance of Mary.

Gratitude is the gift to be given in return for God's great love. We praise Him. We bless Him. We adore Him. We glorify Him. We give Him thanks for His great glory. "How lovely your dwelling, O LORD of hosts!" (Psalm 84:2). Mary's children will always be given the grace to return the love. Those who call upon Mary will find all of her promises passed down from the Father. The promise will be made incarnate through the life of Jesus Christ unto the end of time in us. You are being enriched in every way for all generosity, which through us produces thanksgiving to God" (2 Corinthians 9:11).

Mary conceived and beheld her Son, Jesus. She beholds us, teaches us, nurtures us, and loves us. God will never forget us. His love is brought to life in us. We will never forget Him in return for all that He promised us in the life-giving love found in Jesus. Mary, teach us the Law of Love!

Daily Prayer: Veni Creator, Our Lady of the Blessed Sacrament

Our Lady of the Cenacle

Let us follow our Mother to the Cenacle and listen to the lessons that she there teaches us, lessons that she has received from her Divine Son, with whom she conversed day and night. She is the faithful echo of His heart and of His love. Place yourself under Mary's direction; think her thoughts, speak her words of love, imitate her manners, perform her actions, share her sufferings, and all in her will speak to you of Jesus, of His highest service, of God's greatest glory.

In the cenacle this august Queen kneels as adoratrix and servant of the Most Blessed Sacrament: kneel at your Mother's side and pray with her, and in so doing, you will continue her Eucharistic life on earth.

When you receive Holy Communion, clothe yourself with the virtues and merits of Mary, your Mother, and you will thus communicate with her faith and with her devotion. When you labor to promote the Eucharistic reign of our Lord, unite yourself with Mary's intention and with her joy when she worked for Jesus in the Blessed Sacrament, and you will be happy!

Be humble as Mary-entirely lost in her own nothingness, entirely abandoned to God's grace. Be sweet as Mary. She was the embodiment of the sweetness of the Heart of Jesus. Be devoted as Mary. Mary loved to the extent of Calvary-she loved even unto death. It was on Calvary that she became the Mother of love.

There only will you become a true adorer, worthy of the cenacle, worthy of Jesus and Mary.[53]*- St. Peter Julian*

"She is the faithful echo of His heart and of His love."[54] St. Peter Julian reminds us to be the echo of God's Love in the world. We carry out this voice by imitating the manners of our mother. Mary teaches us day by day the lessons of the law of love at the Altar. We then will have the presence of God within and be clothed in the virtues of her love. This presence can only manifest itself through communicating our own hearts and souls with Jesus, promoting the Eucharistic reign from our entire beings to all whom we encounter. This will be happiness. Mary is the embodiment of Jesus who cries out, "My soul proclaims the greatness of the Lord" (Luke 1:46). Mary is made to be the law of love. She stands in the statutes of God's love as a witness for us to emulate. We then approach and adorn the altar by our love offering to Jesus. We become an echo of God.

St. Peter Julian continues, "she became the Mother of love."[55] What a prominent title for this humble, handmaid of the Lord. Mary is the Mother of the Cenacle, Mother of Love, Mother of God. The Cenacle is where Mary will bring us to become love. It is only at the Cenacle of the Altar where the cenacle of our hearts can meet Divine Love. A true adorer must be nourished here; there is no greater place where the grace of God is found. The Holy Sacrifice of the Mass is the highest form of prayer, where Jesus longs to pour forth His gifts to us through receiving Holy Communion. In the hope that this constant encounter with Him will bring us outside of ourselves

---

[53] Ibid., 104-107.
[54] Ibid.
[55] Ibid.

into the life of God, Mary guides us to Communion, where the law of love is to be found. This grace should mold our charity into thanksgiving; thanksgiving to be shared. We affirm one another in the love that has been given to us. We then echo it to all, "Do you not know that you are the temple of God, and that the Spirit of God dwells in you?" (Colossians 3:16). Mother of Love let the infinite love of Christ pour forth from us unto all of your children.

"Tomorrow will be too late, God calls me now."[56] St. Peter Julian proclaimed these words in his own life. They are words to live by that grant us hope in doing the will of God. A grateful heart will try over and over again to keep sacred the present moment. This moment may be its last moment on earth, so our Eucharistic King grants us the grace of living here and now in His law of love. Tomorrow may be too late, so we do now what we would do if it were our last moment: follow our Mother to the Cenacle. Bringing this home may simply be for us to cast our attention on every person in our lives, being grateful for them, living as if you would never see them again, loving as you will never have the chance to love them again. The cenacle can bring you home to the will of God right where you are in the present moment of your life, right where you live, right where you can make a difference in the Eucharistic Kingdom. The Altar of the Lord with Mary at our side will make us God's delight, a dwelling place for thee. Mary, teach us the law of love. Pray for someone right in your midst that may need prayer and God's love from you.

Daily Prayer: Veni Creator, Our Lady of the Blessed Sacrament

---

[56] Norman Pelletier, SSS, *Tomorrow Will Be Too Late*, (Staten Island, Alba House, 2002), 32.

Life of Adoration in Union with Mary

In considering attentively the reasons that induced our Lord to leave us His Blessed Mother and so separate Himself from her, it seems to me that He did so because He was distrustful of our weakness and inconstancy. He left us His Mother, whose mission it should be to take us by the hand and lead us to His Tabernacle. The Blessed Virgin, then, became our Mother, in view of the Eucharist. To her is entrusted the task of showing us how to find our Bread of Life, she gathered about her a community of pious women at Jerusalem; she dwelt with them, sharing with her treasure of grace and love causing us to take part in her pious devotion to His service-for all that a Mother possesses belongs to her children. Mary being our Mother, then will educate us. The child instinctively goes first to its mother. Our Lord, then, has given us Mary for our Mother, to be pleasing to our Lord, all vocations must pass through Mary's hands.

The mother is the center-she is always the center-we need to dwell always with her, for we need her at all times. She obtains for us every grace; adore our Lord in the company of His Blessed Mother. I do not say abide in Mary. No. Jesus is there before you in order that you may speak to Him direct but do so with Mary; live in her company. Since our Lord has given her to you as directress, never make your adoration without her.

"I repeat to Thee her adoration: for sinners; for the conversion of the world; and for all the needs of the Church!" By doing so you will rejoice in Mary's heart. Oh! If anyone should honor, love

and serve Mary, it is he whose profession it is to live for the Eucharist. Ah! let the Blessed Virgin, then, govern your life; let her lead you to Jesus! She desires but one thing-the glory of her Divine Son and your happiness![57]*- St. Peter Julian*

"To her is entrusted the task of showing us how to find our Bread of Life, she gathered about her a community of pious women at Jerusalem; she dwelt with them, sharing with her treasure of grace and love."[58] St. Peter Julian followed the law of Mary's love in founding the Congregation of the Blessed Sacrament. He lived his life of Adoration in union with Mary. She was St. Peter Julian's directress to the community life. The Congregation, or any order within the Catholic Church, draws you into community life. This is a great gift for those who desire to be part of a family. If the mother governs the family, then the children need to be guided by her to the future of the family's life. We pray with Mary, in union with Mary, and through Mary to her Son. He will lead the way to salvation. "Enter through the narrow gate; for the gate is wide and the road broad that leads to destruction, and those who enter through it are many" (Matthew 7:13). Being led by the hand and heart of Mary is a great comfort to the soul that will free us from all worries. Mary will direct us to the Father who has prepared all things for us perfectly. Our Lady of the Blessed Sacrament will guide us in the law of God's love, His Promise, and His life that will dwell within us.

Individualism is attractive to the humanity we live in. St. Peter Julian reminds us that Jesus knew "He was distrustful of

---

[57] Eymard, *Our Lady of the Blessed Sacrament*, 108-113.
[58] Ibid.

our weakness and inconstancy." [59] God knows we need a mother. We are offered the gift to do all things in and through Mary. We most especially go with Mary in our prayer time; we adore Jesus with her in the Blessed Sacrament. She leads us to trust, so that we may overcome our weakness. She will help us raise our souls to the dignity of life. Mary draws us into community life. The community life draws us into the family of God, which was the intent of our Heavenly Father from all eternity.

> In the beginning, when God created the heavens and the earth—and the earth was without form or shape, with darkness over the abyss and a mighty wind sweeping over the waters—Then God said: Let there be light, and there was light. God saw that the light was good. God then separated the light from the darkness. God called the light "day," and the darkness he called "night." Evening came, and morning followed—the first day (Genesis1:1-5).

We need not worry about the concupiscence of our human weakness. Mary will teach us the law of love. Darkness is over our surface and the depths of us too when we are alone. With the Spirit of God hovering over us from our Baptism, we are drawn into the life of God as His adopted sons and daughters with our mother at our side.

The law of love that leads all into community life as Eucharistic adorers of the Blessed Sacrament, by the hand of Mary, will help us find a place in this family of God. "Let the Blessed Virgin, then, govern your life; let her lead you to Jesus!

---

[59] Ibid.

She desires but one thing-the glory of her Divine Son and your happiness!"[60] Our happiness is found in making a return to Jesus for His life-giving love for us. We find our place to serve in our communities. With different gifts and talents brought together we become whole in the goodness of God. "Some people God has designated in the church to be, first, apostles; second, prophets; third, teachers; then, mighty deeds; then, gifts of healing, assistance, administration, and varieties of tongues" (1Corinthians 12:28). St. Peter Julian continues, "I repeat to Thee her adoration."[61] St. Peter Julian is telling us that he is repeating to Jesus Our Blessed Mother's adoration. Mary's adoration is to pray "for sinners; for the conversion of the world; and for all the needs of the Church. By doing so, you will rejoice in Mary's heart."[62] Praying with Mary to Our Divine Savior will bring each of us into the fullness of community life. She will help us find our place where the need is the greatest and where our gifts will be manifested most. Mary's intentions will become our intentions; her needs for the church will become our needs for the church. The salvation of all will become our duty in union with her.

Our life of Adoration in merging with Mary to serve our Eucharistic Lord Jesus Christ will be a great profit of our love for Him. It is Jesus who takes away the sins of the world and continues to have mercy on us and grant us His peace. Our happiness will be found in our love for Jesus, in offering our daily duties to Jesus through Mary, fulfilling our state in life, and finding our place to serve in God's Holy Mother Church.

---

[60] Ibid.
[61] Ibid.
[62] Ibid.

Mary, teach us the law of love. Pray through Our Lady before Jesus in the Blessed Sacrament to help you find your place of service in our Catholic Church.

Daily Prayer: Veni Creator, Our Lady of the Blessed Sacrament

Mary's Adoration of Faith and Respect

How much might be said of Mary's life of adoration in the Cenacle! Mary was wholly employed in adoring and honoring Him in His Eucharistic life. She prostrated herself with profound respect and devotion, then composed her senses in a simple act of recollection. She kept her body erect, her hands joined or crossed on her breast or, when alone, frequently raised in supplication towards the Tabernacle, on which her eyes were constantly fixed. Mary adored with the most submissive faith. She adored that Heart so inflamed with love, Mary would have wished to annihilate herself completely before the Divine Majesty annihilated in the Sacrament, that by so doing she might render Him due homage and love. Mary's adoration was profound, interior, and intimate. It was the gift of herself. She offered herself wholly to the service of loving God in the Eucharist; for love knows no reservation, lays down no conditions; it thinks no more of self, lives no longer for self; it is a stranger to itself, it lives only for the God whom it loves. All in Mary turned toward the Blessed Sacrament as toward its center and end. A current of grace and love was established between the Adorable Heart of Jesus Hostia and the adoring heart of Mary; they were two flames that burned as one. God was perfectly adored in his creature!

With the example of Mary before him, let the adorer kneel before the Blessed Sacrament with the most profound respect. Under the Eucharistic veils that hide the Sacred Humanity, let us adore Jesus with Mary's faith and with that of Holy Church-those two

Mothers that the Savior has, in His love, given us. Let us adore our God as though we saw Him, heard Him; for an earnest faith sees, hears and touches with more certitude than the senses themselves.[63] – *St. Peter Julian*

We walk with Mary. "Then the two recounted what had taken place on the way and how he was made known to them in the breaking of the bread" (Luke 24:35). Those walking the road to Emmaus must have been in a great state of confusion, wondering, trying to figure out in their minds all that they heard. They listened on the way, they pondered, they thought about how their hearts burned with peace when they recognized Jesus in the breaking of the Bread. St. Peter Julian tells us, "an earnest faith sees, hears and touches with more certitude than the senses themselves."[64] We who believe will find rest for our souls, a comfort, and a peace in finding Jesus in the Blessed Sacrament. Our hearts too will burn with peace. Those on the way continued to wonder, yet their confusion was clear when His presence was before them. We follow Mary through our lives onto the path that will lead us to become fully employed in honoring Jesus in His Eucharistic life.

The Holy Angels, like Mary, the Queen of Angels, simply adore.

All in Mary turned toward the Blessed Sacrament as toward its center and end. A current of grace and love was established between the Adorable Heart of Jesus Hostia and the adoring heart of Mary; they were two

---

[63] Ibid., 114-117.
[64] Ibid.

flames that burned as one. God was perfectly adored in his creature![65]

St. Peter Julian sets before our eyes this imagery. A current of grace can and will be established for us too from the Heart of Jesus in the Blessed Sacrament. With our hearts entering into the union of the hearts of Jesus and Mary, we have a limitless life of grace to long for. We turn over everything to these two hearts, allowing the same current of grace to work through our lives. Mary's example of the law of love will help us find God in losing ourselves so the life of The Heavenly Father can be fulfilled in us. Mary is an example of how to adore with profound respect and devotion. This does not come from a set rule, it comes from our acknowledgement of His love. The return of this love will come from an indwelling of the Holy Spirit in our souls, which will lead us to prostrate ourselves before our King. The prostration is the union of your heart to the Divine Heart, where the two will become one, and a current of grace will unfold.

"Let us, in union with Mary, accompany the Blessed Sacrament when it is taken to the sick".[66] There may be a vast opening of grace offered to us here. "Is anyone among you sick? He should summon the presbyters of the church, and they should pray over him and anoint [him] with oil in the name of the Lord" (James 5:14). There are many sick among us. First, our own hearts are in need of constant nourishment that can only be consoled by the Heart of Jesus Christ in the Blessed Sacrament. Once we have received Jesus, we can offer healing through our prayers to all those suffering in heart, mind, body,

---

[65] Ibid., 115.
[66] Ibid., 117.

and soul. The work will be endless and fall into eternity. "God will be perfectly adored in his creatures."[67] When we care for others, we perfectly adore. Mary will guide us to pray for those in need. God will be perfectly adored when we become more like His Son, who lived and died for us. We will, like Mary, become true adorers in finding Jesus in our lives, making Him its center, and carrying out His work. The vision will be clear that we are heading towards Him. Our Lady of the Blessed Sacrament helps us to become Who we receive so that others may come to magnify the Lord and rejoice in the Word made flesh, Jesus. Mary, teach us the law of love. Pray for someone deeply troubled in heart, mind, body or soul, and offer a hidden sacrifice for their suffering.

Daily Prayer: *Veni Creator*, Our Lady of the Blessed Sacrament

---

[67] Ibid., 115.

Mary's Adoration of Thanksgiving

To her act of humble faith, to her adoration of deep self-annihilation, Mary added thanksgiving. Mary gave thanks to Jesus for His love in the gift of the Eucharist. Oh, how happy Mary was when before the Last Supper Jesus revealed to her that the hour for the triumph of His love had come, that He was about to institute His Adorable Sacrament, by which each of the Faithful could share her happiness and, like her, receive Him into his breast, see Him, after a fashion, and in His Sacramental state enjoy all the graces and experience the mysteries of His mortal life: "After this Gift, in which I exhaust My power, I have nothing more to give to man, except heaven!"

She offered herself to serve Him in His Adorable Sacrament; she consented to delay the hour of her reward, in order that she might remain an adorer on earth, commissioned to guard, to serve the Eucharist, happy to die at the foot of the divine Tabernacle. In her adoration in the Cenacle, Mary daily renewed her thanksgiving: "How good Thou art, my Savior and my Son!" Then Mary gave thanks to each of the powers of Jesus' soul, to each of the Savior's members which had cooperated in the institution of the Eucharist, offering to them the flames of love that consumed her heart.

Oh! how His Heart must have rejoiced at having left Mary His Sacramental Presence for her consolation! Mary's thanksgiving was, furthermore, most agreeable to Jesus because the recognition of benefits received and gratitude of them please Him above all else. That is all He expects from us. To adore by thanksgiving is to adore well. It is to recognize the first of His attributes, the one which above all others He came to earth to manifest- His goodness. Let us dwell at length when we are at His feet. Let us, then return thanks through Mary. A child receives a gift, but it is his mother who thanks the donor for him. So our thanksgiving, united with that of Mary, will be perfect and most acceptable to the Heart of Jesus.[68]- St. Peter Julian

St. Peter Julian tells us of the "flames of love that consumed her heart."[69] Mary was grateful for she was full of grace. "And coming to her, he said, 'Hail, favored one! The Lord is with you'" (Luke 1:28). Mary is in thanksgiving for all of us in honor of the Donor. Our Blessed Mother is full of grace for all of her children. She is full of God's love for us from now until eternity. Jesus is the Donor of love; He gives His life for us continually. "Ask and it will be given to you; seek and you will find; knock and the door will be opened to you" (Matthew 7:7). We ask through Mary, we seek through Mary, and we knock through Mary for the Divine Indwelling of the Holy Spirit to guide us into the fullness of thanksgiving awaiting us in the Blessed Sacrament. Mary's Adoration of thanksgiving will be ours when we offer with her the same flames of love that come from our hearts unto Jesus for all He has given us in His Life. "No one has greater love than this, to lay down one's life for one's friends" (John 15:13). Mary is the first grateful adorer of the Blessed Sacrament; she is full of grace.

---

[68] Ibid., 118-122.
[69] Ibid.

"After this Gift, in which I exhaust My power, I have nothing more to give to man, except heaven!"[70] St. Peter Julian gives an account from his heart, the words of our Savior. Jesus gives his very life for our sins that separate us from the Heavenly Father. He restores us to the fullness of grace. His mercy is without end. "Only goodness and love will pursue me all the days of my life; I will dwell in the house of the LORD for years to come" (Psalm 23:6). Jesus' Mercy will follow us if we follow Him all the days of our life. We need to dwell in the house of the Lord unto the end of our days. Thanksgiving becomes a great part of our prayer time when we are reminded moment by moment of the love of God. Our Blessed Mother's thanks are without end, for she recognized that the Father's Mercy is without end. We knock, we seek, we find Jesus in the Blessed Sacrament. It is there where He longs for us to be with Him. Jesus has nothing more to give except heaven itself. Heaven itself can be found here and now in the Eucharistic Kingdom. We are offered all the fruits and gifts of the Holy Spirit; they are streaming from His Divine presence. We try to remain in a state of grace to receive these offerings, so we can be thankful children. Mary will bring our thanks to Jesus, especially when our pains are greater than our prayers. We find heaven when we seek Jesus, by the law of Mary's love.

St. Peter Julian Eymard instills in us Mary's teaching of the law of love. Week 4 will bring us by Mary's hand into the conclusion of our consecration preparation before we make a promise of our love to Jesus through Our Lady of the Blessed Sacrament. Mary will lead us where this promise will take our hearts: to the adoring of Jesus in the Blessed Sacrament. Our

---

[70] Ibid.

continued prayers to her maternal heart will guide us to follow the will of God. Children of Mary, after silent prayer time, will always be devoted to the Holy Rosary. Praying the scriptures in each mystery brings to mind the Paschal Mystery. This two-fold prayer will bring us into the life of Jesus Christ. The virtues connected to this gift from our mother will always find a way to lead us to Divine Wisdom. Goodness and truth will follow after we enter into the mysteries with a humble and contrite heart. We have so many gifts to be thankful for. The Promise of the Father's love is endless. We live in thanksgiving by loving the gifts that have been given to us, especially, Jesus in the Blessed Sacrament. "Be still and know that I am God! I am exalted among the nations, exalted on the earth" (Psalm 46:11). The Father's Love reigns. We who are blessed to receive Him will have a vision of Heaven from our hearts, united with Mary's Adoration of Thanksgiving, here at the Altar of the Lord, from now into eternity. "Blessed are the peacemakers, for they will be called children of God" (Matthew 5:9). Mary, teach us the law of love. Everything that enters your heart and mind today turn into thanksgiving.

Daily Prayer: Veni Creator, Our Lady of the Blessed Sacrament

WEEK FOUR

THEME: MOTHER OF ADORERS

Intention this week:

Make a perpetual promise to recite a spiritual communion prayer if you cannot get to daily Mass. The faith you place in the prayer is the grace you will receive from it. Continue to journal and prepare for a good and humble confession. Try to find time to spend with Jesus in the Blessed Sacrament. Ponder these words through your prayers this week:

"In your prayer aspire to nourish yourself upon God... This is the secret of true prayer; to discover God's action and plans in His love for us! Then the soul cries out, 'How good you are, oh my God! What can I do for you? What could please you?' That is the flame which rises from the hearth. To attain such a living prayer, we must forget ourselves, or avoid seeking ourselves in any way in prayer. We must simplify the work of our mind by a simple and calm view of God's truths."

-St. Peter Julian Eymard Paris, August 27, 1867

Prayers for each day this week (found in Appendix A)

- Veni Creator
- Litany of the Most Blessed Sacrament

Mary's Eucharistic Contemplation

Contemplation naturally follows adoration and thanksgiving, while at the same time, it nourishes and perfects them. Eucharistic contemplation is the study of Jesus in the Blessed Sacrament, in which the soul considers in detail His marvelous goodness in instituting this Sacrament, studies its motives, examines its sacrifices, weighs its Gift, and appreciates its love.

The soul goes out of self in order to unite with Jesus, in order to adhere to the Divine Object of its contemplation.

Mary's contemplation before the Eucharist was of a nature that no words are adequate to describe. She knew what combats His Heart had to sustain, the sacrifices exacted of Him. The sacrileges of which His Sacrament would be the Object, not only on the part of heretics, but even on the part of his friends; combats of His goodness against the ingratitude of Christians who neglect to receive Him in Holy Communion, refusing thereby His richest graces, His most tender invitation. But the love of Jesus triumphed over all these obstacles: "I shall love men in spite of everything; and their malice can neither discourage nor conquer My goodness!"

In order to appreciate the gift of the Eucharist at Its just value, the adorer ought to go as Mary did, and with her, to Its source, to the sacrifices It demanded of our Lord's love. The contemplation of those combats and of that victory will suggest to the adorer what he owes in return to a God so good. Then, with Mary, His Divine Mother, he will offer himself to Jesus

Eucharistic with his whole heart, to bless him, to thank Him for so much love. He will take Mary as the pattern of his Eucharistic life in order to aid him in his practical study. He will love her and confide himself to her as to the Mother of Adorers, which is the title dearest to her heart and most glorious to Jesus.[71]- St. Peter Julian

---

The most glorious title for Mary is Mother of Adorers. "Do not let your hearts be troubled. You have faith in God; have faith also in me" (John 14:1). Mary's troubled heart at the Annunciation was instantaneously transformed. St. Peter Julian states that "the soul goes out of self to unite with Jesus."[72] Our Lady's belief, "have faith in Me," allowed her soul to go out of itself to unite with Jesus. Would this not be the height of contemplation? There are no words, no adequate explanation, only the adoring heart that could spring forth from this reality.

"The love of God triumphed over all obstacles."[73] Mary's love triumphed with Jesus for she was fully in unison with Him. The Promise of the Father is fulfilled in our belief. Mary shows us the way to believe. We can then try, like her, to adore in the likeness of her as mother. St. Peter Julian is telling us to study Jesus, His goodness, His motives, His sacrifices, His gifts, in appreciation of His love. What do we get from studying Jesus? Where will it bring us in making our consecration promise? St. Peter Julian once again declares words from our Savior, "I shall love men in spite of everything, and their malice can neither discourage nor conquer My

---

[71] Ibid., 123-126.
[72] Ibid., 123.
[73] Ibid., 124.

goodness!"[74] This great saint is reminding us to be like the Mother of Adorers.

"In contrast, the fruit of the Spirit is love, joy, peace, patience, kindness, generosity, faithfulness" (Galatians 5:22). The Mother of Adorers received all wisdom, understanding, counsel, fortitude, knowledge, piety, and fear of the Lord. Mary became all that the Holy Spirit overshadowed her with. Our Blessed Mother's study of Jesus illuminated her existence. Mary was at the height of contemplation. She lived in the beatific vision as she continued to walk the earth. Mother of Adorers raise us to the heights of Heaven! St. Peter Julian adds, "In order to appreciate the gift of the Eucharist at its just value, the adorer ought to go as Mary did, and with her, to Its source, to the sacrifices It demanded of our Lord's love."[75] Along with all the blessings of the Holy Spirit, we are called to sacrifice. When we can sacrifice and have true joy in the offering, we find motherhood in adoring.

"The angel said to them, "Do not be afraid; for behold, I proclaim to you good news of great joy that will be for all the people"" (Luke 2:10). If Mary is aiding us in this practical study, we will be put to the test. "Test everything; retain what is good" (1 Thessalonians 5:21).

We have the freedom to believe in all of the gifts. By the power of the Holy Spirit coming from the pursuit of Jesus, we must never lose sight of our freedom. Our contemplation with Mary can only offer us a pass into the grace available to us in following our new formed conscience. Every choice we make needs to be guided by the fruits and gifts of the Holy Spirit, by the heart of Mary, and through the presence of Jesus in the

---

[74] Ibid., 124.
[75] Ibid.

Eucharist. This is poured out for us in the Paschal Mystery gifts. With Mary, we offer her Fiat for the unfolding of our souls so that they may be filled with the Holy Spirit. Mother of Adorers, who let this be done unto you according to God's Word, please lead us in the way of salvation. "And the angel said to her in reply, "The holy Spirit will come upon you, and the power of the Most High will overshadow you. Therefore, the child to be born will be called holy, the Son of God" (Luke 1:35).

Examine the state of joy in your life.

Daily Prayer: Veni Creator, Litany of the Most Blessed Sacrament

Week 4 - Day 2

Mary's Adoration of Propitiation

Mary adored her very dear Son in His character of Victim immolated perpetually on our Altars, incessantly imploring grace and mercy for sinners, through the merits of His death. Mary adoring her God present on the altar by the Consecration, shed abundant tears: at the sight of those who make no account of this august Sacrifice, and so render fruitless this Mystery of their Redemption. Mary would willingly have offered a thousand deaths to repair so many outrages; poor Mother! Is not one Calvary sufficient for her? Why renew her sorrows daily and pierce her heart anew with words of impiety?

However, Mary, as the best of Mothers, instead of rejecting and cursing these sinners, took upon herself the penalty of their crimes; she expiated them by suffering; she herself became a victim at the foot of the altar, imploring grace and mercy for her guilty children. Mary adored Jesus in the state of Prisoner which Jesus assumed by uniting Himself inseparably to the Sacred Species.

"O happy bonds that keep Jesus in our midst," said Mary," be ye blessed! It is love that keeps you here, and forever, in order that I may make of Jesus my Treasure, my Prisoner of love, the Companion of my captivity here below, the God of my heart!" Mary adored the hidden state of Jesus' Divinity and Humanity in His Sacrament, veiled that man might not attach himself to the glory and beauty of his person. Jesus thus veiled Himself only to spiritualize man's faith, to purify his heart, to stimulate his

love, and to attract him to the Infinite, to an ever new and ever-increasing beauty.

Mary honored the hidden life of Jesus by a retired and solitary life. She passed the greater part of her time in making reparation for ungrateful man.

He loved the sacrifices that He had so generously made, and He preferred His state of annihilation to that of His glory. Mary, His Mother and the Mother of all adorers, made amends to Him for everything, and the love of Jesus found inexpressible satisfaction in receiving her prayers, and her tears shed for the salvation of the world.[76]- St. Peter Julian

"Mary, His Mother and the Mother of all adorers, makes amends to Him for everything, and the love of Jesus found inexpressible satisfaction in receiving her prayers, and her tears shed for the salvation of the world."[77] This is our continued life in the Catholic Church, to make amends to Jesus for everything He has given us. There is no way out until the end of our days.

Simon Peter answered him, "Master, to whom shall we go? You have the words of eternal life" (John 6:68).

If we look at the practice above, we can see that we are being asked by Our Mother to assist at Mass and frequently remunerate for those who fail to fulfill this command of the Church. We who follow the Mother of Adorers must save the whole family of God by our participation. "I say unto you, that he will avenge them speedily. Nevertheless, when the Son of man cometh, shall he find faith on the earth?" (Luke 18:8).

---

[76] Ibid., 127-131.
[77] Ibid., 130.

Jesus will find faith on earth through Our Lady's consecrated children, who will be before the Blessed Sacrament when Jesus comes again. "He will come again to judge the living and the dead."[78] Mary's adoration of propitiation will live through her children. Jesus in the Blessed Sacrament will find inexpressible satisfaction in receiving our prayers and tears for the salvation of the world. St. Peter Julian cries out with these words, "Poor Mother! Is not one Calvary sufficient for her?"[79] Mary too will be consoled when her loving children are with her in the celebration of Holy Mass. There will be an inexpressible gift of love returned to Jesus for His life-giving love for us.

If we take flight into the Holy Rosary and think of why certain mysteries are set forth for us to pray, we may find after offering our Hail Mary's over and over, a thread of graces flowing through to connect the whole life of Christ. The Rosary is given as an inexpressible gift of love to God. This is Mary's requested atonement for us, to pray the scriptures. To offer the intercession of our prayers, with the Mother of Adorers, to Jesus. Only the infinite Wisdom of God could send this thread of grace through the virtues connected to the Holy Rosary, encompassing the whole life of Christ. If we prayerfully ponder the Second Mystery in each set of the Mysteries of the Holy Rosary, we see how Mary's Son instructs us to act according to her love.

We begin with the Second Joyful Mystery, The Visitation. Our Lady comes out of herself to aid another. Elizabeth rejoiced with the Holy Spirit. Leaping in her womb, the love is passed, received, and new life comes forth from St. John the

---

[78] Nicene Creed.
[79] Eymard, *Our Lady of the Blessed Sacrament*, 128.

Baptist. A perfect charity is fulfilled in The Visitation. We pray for the same grace upon our lives, a perfect charity towards our neighbor.

The thread continues with the Second Sorrowful Mystery, The Scourging. We pray for the grace to mortify our senses to perfection.

Yet it was our pain that he bore, our sufferings he endured. We thought of him as stricken, struck down by God and afflicted, But he was pierced for our sins, crushed for our iniquity. He bore the punishment that makes us whole, by his wounds we were healed (Isaiah 53: 4-5).

When we immerse ourselves in the pain that Jesus embraced for love of us, with each lash of the whips, we can only re-reflect on The Visitation and the perfect charity that will come by the grace of God when we offer our scourging to Him. Our mortifications, offered with a humble and contrite heart, will find the mercy of God. Only then, from this pure offering, will we see God. "Blessed are the clean of heart, for they will see God" (Matthew 5:8).

We move on to The Second Luminous Mystery, The Wedding Feast at Cana. Just as He changed the water into wine, Jesus transfers His fidelity to make our lives rich and faithful in His Blood through the contribution of our lives. We offer ourselves in return for the gift given by His Blood. We are wed to the altar of the Lamb of God who has come to take away our sins.

Finally, on The Second Glorious Mystery, Jesus reveals His Ascension into Heaven. Silently trusting in Jesus, our offerings of charity, fidelity, and mortification bring us into the Divine Wisdom of the Heavenly Father. The Ascension is where we pray for a great hope and longing for Heaven, where our own life in these mysteries of our salvation will, by the grace of God, lead us to Heaven.

St. Peter Julian reminds us, "Mary honored the hidden life of Jesus by a retired and solitary life. She passed the greater part of her time in making reparation for ungrateful man."[80] May our prayers united to the intentions of Mary bring pardon to those who are lost, those who are lonely, and those who do not believe. The Paschal Mystery will keep our hearts ready for Christ who will come again. Mary's propitiation will be ours. We become one with the Trinity by going with Her to the Mystical Table where we receive her Son, Jesus! In "Mary's Adoration of Propitiation"[81] we, her loving and trustful children, pray without ceasing for God's goodness to reign. "Pray without ceasing" (1 Thessalonians 5:17).

In the final days of the consecration preparation, we look for the ways Our Lady will continue to unfold gifts in our lives. We need to cling to the Eucharist, Sacramentally or Spiritually, by receiving Jesus daily. Pray the Holy Rosary if you are able. Set a routine and try to be obedient to it without falling into guilt. If you are pulled from it, simply begin again. Make a good and humble confession, offering it for your consecration promise sometime within the upcoming week. Continue to let the reflections enter your heart. Pray on the words that are prominent to you. How can you apply them to your life right now, and what do you think God is asking of you in the Word? Mary is the Mother of Adorers. We are her children who fall not far from her maternal care. Mary will always lead us to live in Jesus Christ, who suffered and died to give us the everlasting

---

[80] Ibid.
[81] Ibid.

love of God Our Father. St. Peter Julian asks us to assist at Mass, attend Mass as often as we are able, to unite with Our Lady, and to be one with her who is the Mother of Adorers. "Mary adored her very dear Son in His character of Victim immolated perpetually on our Altars, incessantly imploring grace and mercy for sinners, through the merits of His death."[82] (St Peter Julian)

> And the angel said to her in reply, "The holy Spirit will come upon you, and the power of the Most High will overshadow you. Therefore the child to be born will be called holy, the Son of God" (Luke 1:35).

Let us pray this day for the grace to mortify our senses to the sensitivity of God's Wisdom.

Daily Prayer: Veni Creator, Litany of the Most Blessed Sacrament

---

[82] Ibid.

Mary's Prayer of Adoration

Mary devoted herself exclusively to the Eucharistic glory of Jesus. She knew it was the desire of the Eternal Father to make the Eucharist known, loved and served by all men; that the need of Jesus' Heart was to communicate to all men His gifts of grace and glory. She knew, too, that it was the mission of the Holy Spirit to extend and perfect in the hearts of men the reign of Jesus Christ, and that the Church had been founded only to give Jesus to the world.

She was consumed with the desire to make Jesus in the Blessed Sacrament known to all, to inflame all hearts with His love, to see them enchained to His loving service. In her boundless zeal, she embraced the needs of the Faithful everywhere, for all time to come, who would inherit the Holy Eucharist and be Its adorers.

But the mission dearest to Mary's heart was that of constant prayer for the success of the preaching and the missionary labors of the Apostles and of all the members of Jesus Christ's priesthood. It is not surprising, then, that those Apostolic workers so easily converted entire kingdoms, for Mary remained constantly at the foot of the Throne of Mercy, supplicating on their behalf the Savior's benevolence. Her prayers converted countless souls. "Blessed is he for whom Mary prays!"

Eucharistic adorers share Mary's life and mission of prayer at the foot of the Most Blessed Sacrament. It is, moreover, the most necessary to the Church. We must have souls who by their importunity re-open the treasures of grace. We must have true adorers; that is to say, men of fervor and of sacrifice. Mary's apostolate, moreover, consisted in the very persuasive preaching of example. Any negligence in dress or carelessness of manner on his part would indicate little faith and a disorderly interior. Respect in the holy place, above all before the Most Holy Sacrament, ought to be the characteristic exterior virtue of adorers.

Jesus Christ-for example is the royal lesson of wisdom and most fruitful apostolate.[83]*- St. Peter Julian*

"Blessed is he for whom Mary prays!"[84] Imagine that Mary's prayer of adoration brought someone to pass the Catholic faith onto us. We can be sure Our Blessed Mother was with them on our behalf, at our Baptism and continued Sacramental life. Whether you were baptized as an infant or later in life, our Mother had a share in that entrance into the life of the Heart of her Son.

"Enter through the narrow gate; for the gate is wide and the road broad that leads to destruction, and those who enter through it are many" (Matthew 7:13).

The narrow gate is a dedication to Jesus Christ in the Blessed Sacrament. Mary "devoted herself exclusively to the Eucharistic glory of Jesus." We who are given the grace, are called to prepare ourselves to receive Communion as if it would be our first or our last time. We are called to be, as much as possible, at the throne of mercy before the Blessed Sacrament. St. Peter Julian guides our thoughts to the mission as Adorers of the Blessed Sacrament. He says, "Eucharistic

---

[83] Ibid., 132-137.
[84] Ibid.

adorers share Mary's life and mission of prayer at the foot of the Most Blessed Sacrament."[85] The intercession of our prayers united to the heart of the Mother of Adorers will continue to bring success to the endeavors of missions, priests, and all members of the Catholic Church. Mary's consecrated children share in her intentions. We trust in where this Mother of Mercy will offer them first. Mother of Adorers guide us to be like you. Instill in our hearts the truth that nothing can separate us from the love of God. "Nor height, nor depth, nor any other creature will be able to separate us from the love of God in Christ Jesus our Lord" (Romans 8:39).

At this point in our preparation, we unite the scriptures in particular to the Most Holy Rosary. The thread found through each Third Mystery can only once again be provided for us by Divine Wisdom. In the Third Joyful Mystery, The Birth of Jesus, we pray for a detachment from the things of this world. Nothing is more important than Jesus Christ being born for us, nothing more sacred than a precious child, nothing reveals God more to us than life. We rejoice in the glorious gift God gives us in children. We are blessed to have them either physically or spiritually; "I prayed for this child, and the LORD granted my request" (1 Samuel 1:27). Every second is a gift of precious time loaned to us for a while, so we pray for a detachment from all things of this world to focus on the gift of life.

In the Third Sorrowful Mystery, the Crowning with Thorns, we offer our prayer for a profound humility and trust. The Birth of Christ, who was born in the most humble place with the trust of His parents, is brought to the fullness of this

---

[85] Ibid.

life of trust in the Father. This life of trust magnifies the true power of God when the mockery of men looks into the face of mercy and chooses evil. Our humility offered in silence to the Heavenly Father when we are called to be humble in the face of evil, is a grace that can only be carried out from the divine connection to the Heart of God. When Jesus was crowned with thorns he looked up to His Father and did not utter a word. His trust was all that was needed. His pain was not in vain, only withheld from glory until the Promise of the Father would be revealed for the offering. In the Crowning with Thorns, there is a trust that can only be extended to us by the Triune God. In the birth, we find humility and trust. In the Crowning with Thorns, we find humility and trust.

The string of the third mysteries is continued in the Third Luminous Mystery, the Proclamation of the Kingdom of Heaven. In this mystery we pray for a desire for holiness, connecting to true humility. God, the Father, is proclaimed by the continuous humble service breathed through the life of His Son.

Coming into the fullness of God's gifts, we are given the Third Glorious Mystery. Here, the fire of God's Love with the Descent of the Holy Spirit is upon us. The Merciful Heart of Our Creator will grasp the humble offerings as an entrance into the magnitude of the great descent in the power of the Almighty. God will never forsake us. He did not forsake His Son. His time is endless, and His Glory is revealed by an infinite Wisdom that is beyond our wants and fears. "Then the peace of God that surpasses all understanding will guard your hearts and minds in Christ Jesus" (Philippians 4:7).

St. Peter Julian shares,

But the mission dearest to Mary's heart was that of constant prayer for the success of the preaching and the missionary labors of the Apostles and of all the members of Jesus Christ's priesthood. It is not surprising, then, that those Apostolic workers so easily converted entire kingdoms, for Mary remained constantly at the foot of the Throne of Mercy, supplicating on their behalf the Savior's benevolence. Her prayers converted countless souls. Blessed is he for whom Mary prays![86]

Our prayer begins before the Eucharistic Lord, and it extends through our Rosaries, living or recited. The offering of our daily duties will keep the Gospel alive in the Savior's benevolence, goodness will be manifested in our lives.

Keep your consecration preparation alive by making a conscious effort to offer the readings and reflections through Our Lady of the Blessed Sacrament. Remember we are preparing to make a promise, a promise to enter more deeply into the will of God for our lives. We strive to obtain a good prayer routine, however, if your day is filled with unusual surprises, the offering of your will to God's Will is the gift you can offer for the day. If the only thing you do in a day is receive Jesus in Holy Communion, you have done everything. Embrace the offering of a Spiritual Communion prayer if you cannot get to daily Mass. If it is a day that you cannot even recite a formal prayer you can simply ask, "Jesus although I cannot receive you sacramentally, please come spiritually into my heart as if I have received You." Then take some time to be with Jesus, and you will be keeping your dedication to the

---

[86] Ibid.

Blessed Sacrament alive, nourished, and real. Consecrating your life is to enter more fully into the mystery of Christ. Our lives will become a living prayer. Our happiness will be found through our lives in this mystery of Christ. Mary's prayer of adoration will permeate our existence. Our lives will be blessed by the Eucharistic love that we will have in Jesus Christ. St. Peter Julian says, "she was consumed with the desire to make Jesus in the Blessed Sacrament known to all, to inflame all hearts with His love, to see them enchained to His loving service."[87] Mary Mother of Adorers, teach us to pray!

"Mary adored her very dear Son in His character of Victim immolated perpetually on our Altars, incessantly imploring grace and mercy for sinners, through the merits of His death."[88]

> And the angel said to her in reply, "The Holy Spirit will come upon you, and the power of the Most High will overshadow you. Therefore the child to be born will be called holy, the Son of God" (Luke 1:35).

Reach out to someone who you know may hurt you again with a simple message that you are praying for them.

Daily Prayer: Veni Creator, Litany of the Most Blessed Sacrament

---

[87] Ibid.
[88] Ibid., 127.

Mary's Apostolate

The soul that lives on the Eucharist ought to occupy itself, before everything else, with the interests of this Adorable Sacrament. Now the first and dearest of all these interests to Jesus is His priesthood. It is through the priest that the Blessed Sacrament is given to us. By priests, Jesus receives that sacramental life which He consecrates to the glory of His Father; by them, He has given them all His rights and all His power.

Pray, therefore, for the priesthood; beg for vocations to it may be multiplied; labor to obtain holy, zealous priests for people. This was Mary's prayer; the priest is Mary's privileged child. The priest formed by Mary! - O good and holy priest, how well Jesus will receive thee!

The priest is the father of Jesus Eucharistic, the spiritual king of souls: he is a god on earth, terrenus Deus, who has received all the riches of God- who opens and closes heaven.

The mission and the duties of the priest in regard to the Eucharist and in regard to souls are the same as those of Mary. The priest is, first of all, an adorer and the guardian of the Blessed Sacrament. He must begin at the foot of the altar his exterior apostolate. Mary in the Cenacle! Behold the Divine Mother in her first duty. Her office there is that of an adorer. She adores by taking care of the Eucharistic worship. She repairs the glory of God outraged by sinners.

Behold the faithful priest- one who understands the favor of the Savior's love for him- owes to Jesus!

She revealed the mysteries of His life to the Apostles and the Evangelists. She spoke incessantly of Him and made Him loved by all around. She was the first zealatrix of Jesus.

She loves them (Priests) for the glory of God and the salvation of souls. If we love the Eucharist, if we desire to have It served, preached, loved by all, let us incessantly beg of Jesus, through Mary, to give us holy priests, apostolic workers, faithful adorers. The glory of the Blessed Sacrament and the salvation of the world are at stake.[89]- St. Peter Julian

"The priest is Mary's privileged child."[90]

St. Peter Julian Eymard understands the mission and duty of the sacred priesthood. He understands the immense importance of priests held by Our Blessed Mother. Our Lady knows Jesus receives His Sacramental Life, which He glorifies to the Father, through the priesthood. We as her consecrated children have an obligation to pray fervently for priests, to restore any dignity that may be lost due to our humanity. We can consider it a grievous sin to engage in gossip about a priest. Offer to pray if anyone suggests conversation of one. If you feel you need to find a good and holy confessor to confide in, do so, but never engage in talk with others, rather pray. For the hands of the priest confect the Eucharist at the altar of the Lord through the power of Almighty God. This is the epitome of gifts this side of Heaven. We pray for our priests, for they are the ones who open and close the door to Heaven. Mary's Apostolate was graced with the knowledge that her priests stand in the person of her Son during the Mass. She holds them

---

[89] Ibid., 138-143.
[90] Ibid.

as her privileged children. Souls who live on the Eucharist must treasure the sacred priesthood and occupy with Mary, the Mother of Adorers, the intercession of our love for our priests, for their mission, and for their duties.

St. Peter Julian reminds us that, "She reveals the mysteries of His life."[91] We should offer our daily rosary for priests. Meditating on the Fourth Mystery of each set of Mysteries, we begin with the Fourth Joyful Mystery, the Presentation of Jesus in the Temple. In this mystery, we pray for purity of heart, mind, body, soul, and for obedience. Mary brings her priests to the temple to offer them this grace.

The Carrying of the Cross, the next in the thread of Fourth Mysteries, obliges us to pray for patience amongst our sufferings. Purity will bring us here, for we begin to understand the offering and the grace that will come from carrying our sorrows. The saints grasped this gift and longed for sacrifices to offer, desiring graces to come down upon them.

We remember the Transfiguration, the Fourth Luminous Mystery, at every Holy Mass, recalling Mount Tabor. This is our consolation in the Eucharistic Lord. We too would only want to say like St. Peter, "Lord, it is good that we are here. If you wish, I will make three tents here, one for you, one for Moses, and one for Elijah" (Matthew 17:4), yet the mission of our lives needs to be fulfilled. We face crosses, toils, and disappointments. We need the altar (Mount Tabor) to remember when we are in the face of evils, that Jesus will raise us back to the mountaintop in the illumination of His graces received in Holy Communion. Jesus will remind us of the Father's words,

---

[91] Ibid., 141.

115

While he was still speaking, behold, a bright cloud
cast a shadow over them, then from the cloud came a
voice that said, "This is my beloved Son, with whom
I am well pleased; listen to him. (Matthew 17:5)

We move on to the Fourth Glorious Mystery, The
Assumption. This is the most glorious reminder that God will
never be outdone in His generosity. Our Blessed Mother was
assumed from her pain, taken by the love of her Father to
Heaven. To know Jesus through Our Lady of the Most Blessed
Sacrament will reveal all the mysteries of Jesus Christ to our
hearts and souls. Mary's Apostolate will live on in her children,
and Jesus Eucharistic will be with us unto the end of the world.
"The priest is the father of Jesus Eucharist."[92] St. Peter Julian's
love for his own divine office is a passion of his love for the
Blessed Sacrament, for he knows the priest is needed to
continue the life of Christ in God's Holy Mother Church. St.
Peter Julian knows too that we need to pray for our Lady to
continue to form relationships with her priests for, "she was the
first zealatrix of Jesus."[93] Zealatrix is a serious word for a
serious mission. Mary's mission is our mission. We pray with
her for the most sacred and high office this side of Heaven,
which lives in God's priests. The indelible mark placed upon
the soul of a priest is the mark that consecrates the Eucharistic
sacrifice. Mary's duty is appointed to her by God the Father to
behold her priests. God's promise is fulfilled in the redemptive
life of His Son, Jesus Christ. Our Blessed Mother was the
privileged one to bring Jesus into the world. God chose no
other way than through the heart, life, soul, and womb of the

---

[92] Ibid.
[93] Ibid.

Blessed Virgin Mary. The priests live in Jesus' person, in persona Christi. Mary too must keep them in her heart, soul, life, and womb. The same way she carried Jesus. The children carry out the mission of the family, so we with Mary honor the sacred priesthood. We restore by our love anything humanity may have shattered. The priest is the father of the Eucharist. We need to pray for good and holy priests. Mother of Adorers help us to pray for, "The glory of the Blessed Sacrament and the salvation of the world are at stake."[94] Our Lady of the Blessed Sacrament your apostolate is ours, teach us to be like you the Mother of Adorers.

> And the angel said to her in reply, "The holy Spirit will come upon you, and the power of the Most High will overshadow you. Therefore the child to be born will be called holy, the Son of God" (Luke 1:35).

Pray with Our Lady of the Blessed Sacrament for priests. Try to identify with them all the duties of their life and offer a hidden sacrifice for the gift of their love.

Daily Prayer: Veni Creator, Litany of the Most Blessed Sacrament

---

[94] Ibid.

The Divine Spouse and King of the Heart

In her adoration, Mary aimed at honoring all the different states of Jesus, at exalting Him under His dearest titles, those which establish most perfectly His empire over men's hearts.

She adored Jesus in His capacity of spouse of souls. Union is the end of love. Jesus is a jealous God. The soul, His spouse, must live for Him alone. Woe to him that steals from Jesus the spouse of His Heart!

At Cana she prevented the embarrassment of the bride and bridegroom, so does she adorn the faithful soul with her own virtues, in order that Jesus may find it less unworthy of Him.

And though Mother of the Church, she was at the same time her daughter, and like the most submissive of her children, she obeyed Peter and John and all priests. She adored Jesus through the Church; through her worship, her liturgical prayers, her priesthood, in company with her children. Beautiful adoration was that which united Mary and the faithful at the foot of the Most Blessed Sacrament. Mary adored Jesus as King, for the Holy Eucharist the Savior's royalty. Truth to triumph over men must pass through the Eucharist, in order to catch some of Its sweetness. Jesus, then, is the King of truth through the Eucharist.

Oh, what sighs, what prayers for the Eucharistic reign of Jesus issued from Mary's heart in the Cenacle! The Eucharist spreading and the love of Jesus triumphing everywhere. At last, Jesus will be loved, His Eucharist will find everywhere sympathetic hearts; Its fire will envelop the world and by so doing will completely renew it. O, Divine King! May Thy truth be my ensign of honor; Thy virtues, my shield of defense; Thy love, my word of command; and Thy greater Eucharistic glory, the fruit of my victory! This is the ardent prayer of my heart, which I offer Thee through Mary, the Queen of the Cenacle, and the Mother of Adorers.[95] - *St. Peter Julian*

St. Peter Julian Eymard tells us that Jesus is the Divine Spouse and King of the Heart.

So stand fast with your loins girded in truth, clothed with righteousness as a breastplate, and your feet shod in readiness for the gospel of peace. In all circumstances, hold faith as a shield, to quench all [the] flaming arrows of the evil one. And take the helmet of salvation and the sword of the Spirit, which is the word of God (Ephesians 6:14-17).

The living Word of God is our virtue and shield of defense, the sword of the spirit, and our helmet of salvation. St. Peter Julian in his Eucharistic mindset says this, "Truth to triumph over men must pass through the Eucharist."[96] We find this truth in the Living Bread that comes down from Heaven. We sit, we open our minds, and we try to listen after unlocking our hearts, so the mind and heart may meet to catch some of its sweetness. The Word of God is alive.

Indeed, the word of God is living and effective, sharper than any two-edged sword, penetrating even

---

[95] Ibid. 144-148.
[96] Ibid.

between soul and spirit, joints and marrow, and able to discern reflections and thoughts of the heart (Hebrews 4:12).

What a great gift we have in the scriptures. We make Jesus the Divine Spouse of our hearts when we listen to all He has pledged to us. How our hearts long to be one with the Word, who has been made flesh and dwells among us. The fire of God's love will envelop the world, and the Eucharistic reign will triumph. God's people long to hear His voice. His voice will call them to the healing power of His Eucharistic Kingdom. Our Lady of the Blessed Sacrament adores Jesus in the liturgical prayers. She too hears His voice in the company of her children. Mary unites with us at the foot of the Blessed Sacrament. Jesus, Divine Spouse and King of the Heart, help us to hear your voice in the depths of our longing for Your peace.

God's love is evident as we follow each Fifth Mystery of the Most Holy Rosary, where we continue to find unending graces flowing in the virtues of our Heavenly Father's love. Faithful and true is our God when we pray for fidelity in the Finding of Jesus in the Temple, the Fifth Joyful Mystery. Fidelity connects to this day's title: Jesus is the Divine spouse and King of the heart who remains in the Tabernacles of the world, loyal to His loved ones. Jesus leads us by His example, leaving the crowd to be in His Father's house, revealing to us our first call to serve God, a jealous God, who patiently waits for our love. We continue to find Jesus in the temple. Jesus, truly present in the Blessed Sacrament, desiring to give us His living Word, reflects His life to us by the virtues that stream out of His Eucharistic Heart.

There is so much to pray upon in the Fifth Sorrowful Mystery, The Crucifixion of Our Lord and Savior Jesus Christ. We ponder this greatest of mysteries by simply begging Him for our faithfulness from the Finding in the Temple to the cross of His Love. The Crucifixion, the Redemption of our fallen nature is restored by the sacrifice of Christ's life. Jesus' faithful love to the Heavenly Father when he was found in the Temple is the same faithful love He offers in the ultimate sacrifice of humility, calling out from the Cross for us to return love, to die to self so to live for others. From ages past the faithful have found Divine Wisdom in gazing upon the Cross of Christ. The love Jesus poured upon us is the love He longs for in return.

Jesus does not leave us at the cross of His life or ours. Jesus leaves us The Institution of the Holy Eucharist. In the Fifth Luminous Mystery, we give thanksgiving to Our Eucharistic Lord who remains with us in Holy Communion. The Blessed Sacrament is the living truth that will help us to be faithful servants to God, who will bless us with His promised glory.

The same glory is finally reflected when Our Blessed Mother is crowned Queen of Heaven and earth in the Fifth Glorious Mystery. The Promise of the Heavenly Father adorns His beloved daughter for her life-giving service in the likeness of Her Son. We, her consecrated children, who belong to Our Lady of the Blessed Sacrament, will become spouses to our Lord and Savior, Jesus Christ, by offering, like Mary, our lives to Him.

We are left with this practice, "We should pray constantly to Mary to extend the Eucharistic reign of Jesus Christ throughout the whole world." [97] The practice lives on by praying. Praying with Mary before the Blessed Sacrament, praying with Mary in our Rosaries, along with all of our other prayerful devotions, this is where we find a life that will never end. The grace of our prayers will unfold to the end of our days here on earth. Our lives will rejoice in our Savior. God longs to reign in our hearts. We can change the course of salvation for the glory of God and His goodness through the intercession of our prayers. Prayer changes things according to His Divine Will. We find Jesus in our fidelity and in our own crucifixions. We find Him even more when we die to self and live for others. We need the nourishment of the Holy Eucharist upon the reception of Holy Communion. The continuous prayers we offer will keep us in the luminous love of God. We too will be crowned like Mary at the end of our days if we persevere to the end like our good Mother, who received her crown by the perseverance of her own self-annihilation. Our union with Mary will keep us loving her as Queen and Mother, who will keep us in the truth and honor of Jesus. "May thy truth be my ensign of honor; greater Eucharistic glory, the fruit of my victory! This is the ardent prayer of my heart, which I offer Thee through Mary, the Queen of the Cenacle, and the Mother of Adorers."[98]

With Jesus as King of your heart reach out to someone who may need to hear His voice through you.

Daily Prayer: Veni Creator, Litany of the Most Blessed Sacrament

---

[97] Ibid., 148.
[98] Ibid., 147.

The Eucharist, the Center of Mary's Life

Mary shared the Eucharistic life of Jesus. Love desires a life in common with the Beloved. She had always shared His life of suffering, consequently with good reason she would live the Eucharistic life of her Divine Son, which is the crown of all the others. Mary lived, by means of the Eucharist, a life altogether interior and hidden, silent, separated from the world, with Jesus for her only witness and confidant. She had but one desire, to love Him still more, "My heart and my flesh have rejoiced in God, my Savior."

This Eucharistic contemplation is more active than passive. It is the soul giving itself incessantly to God, under the ever new and ever livelier impression of His goodness, under the ever-increasing action of the flames of His love, which purifies it, detaches it from all earthly things, and unites it more intimately with the Well-Beloved. Prolonged prayer costs little or nothing because freed from all things, it can follow its Savior whithersoever He goes; nothing urging or calling it elsewhere, it can then study the profound mysteries on which it meditates. It sees things as they really are in Jesus Christ; recollection and contemplation strengthen its sight and render it reflective and penetrating.

Perfect must have been Mary's contemplation before the Blessed Sacrament, with the great light of her faith, the purity of her life, the perfect love of her heart. (Mary) drank in long droughts of living waters of grace and of love. She forgot the world about her in order to remain alone with Jesus; for it is a characteristic of love to isolate itself more closely to the beloved. Let the adorer, united to Mary Adoratrix, apply himself with patience, with constancy, to the virtue of recollection, to the exercise of the contemplation of Jesus Christ; studying at first to know Him rather than enjoy Him; for love comes of truth known, and the grace of enlightenment is of more value than the greatest grace of sweetness and consolation. Truth remains, but sentiment passes.

Oh, happy the soul which penetrates, as Mary did, the sublimity of this mystery of love, who desires it, who asks it without ceasing, who incessantly exercises itself in it! The Kingdom of God is within it![99]*- St. Peter Julian*

Mary, "had but one desire, to love Him still more, 'My heart and my flesh have rejoiced in God, my Savior.'"[100] With these words St. Peter Julian is preparing us for life after our consecration preparation. Where do we go from here? Our lives need to remain in common with the Beloved. Our Lady's commonality is to continuously share in the suffering of her children, to rejoice with them, and to live in the depths of the heart of Christ with them. We, her consecrated children, like our Mother who adores, will share in the sufferings of the whole body of Christ as we adore Him in the Blessed Sacrament. The sorrows of others become ours. We hope the intercession of our prayers will bring consolation. "If [one] part suffers, all the parts suffer with it; if one part is honored, all the parts share its joy" (1 Corinthians 12:26).

In our Eucharistic relationship with Jesus, we shall receive a confidant and friend that will be everlasting. We too

---

[99] Ibid., 149-153.
[100] Ibid.

will become sanctified by our hidden, silent life, a life separated from this world. We will become active rather than passive, for the love we absorb from Jesus will not be kept. Our life in God will become an offering. We "isolate" our security by purifying and strengthening our relationship in prayer, allowing it to be reflective and penetrating to all those we encounter; "It is a characteristic of love to isolate itself more closely to the beloved."[101] Mary gathers her children in her likeness. We try to make the Eucharist the center of our lives. With Jesus as our center, He will become our spiritual food: Jesus Eucharistic, our confidant, and friend!

St. Peter Julian tells us, "happy the soul which penetrates, as Mary did, the sublimity of this mystery of love." [102] The mysteries of Mary's love remain in her gift of the Most Holy Rosary- praying the Scriptures, the life of her Son, Jesus Christ. With hope our Consecration preparation will embrace the importance of our continued life in Christ by keeping the Rosary, after our Eucharistic prayer time, sacred. We conclude the little insight we have touched on by reflecting on each First Mystery of the Holy Rosary. The first shall be last, as Matthew says, "Thus, the last will be first, and the first will be last" (Matthew 20:16).

The First Joyful Mystery is The Annunciation of the Lord. The Incarnation of Jesus Christ sustains us with His life when we receive Him, for He lives on in us. We announce Him to the world. Jesus calls us like Mary to humble service.

At the Agony in the Garden of Gethsemane, the First Sorrowful Mystery, Jesus fulfills the Incarnation by handing His life freely to the Divine Will. Mary's humility at the

---

[101] Ibid.
[102] Ibid.

Annunciation is not left without consolation. It is rather blessed all the greater with the conquering of our original sin. Jesus' agony restores our life in the Promise of God our Father. Pride is taken by humility, selfishness is conquered by love, and love is offered to redeem us. The blood Jesus sweat is given to strengthen us to stay with Him one hour.[103] Pray and make a promise to commit to a weekly Holy Hour after your consecration day. This would be a gift of love offered to God.

We pray next the First Luminous Mystery, the Baptism of Jesus in the River Jordan. This is our entrance into the family of God. We must keep our Baptismal promise alive by our Eucharistic dedication. Jesus and the Father are one; we too are one with the Father through Baptism our life in the Blessed Sacrament. We are His beloved children, who are not abandoned but loved. Our Eucharistic life should bring us into the life of the Triune God, where all of our security exists in the reality that we are beloved children of the Father, in and through the life of the Son, sanctified by the Holy Spirit.

Finally, we arrive at the First Glorious Mystery. The Resurrection is our theological life of faith, hope, and love. Here our continued consecrated life is taken to an experienced life of faith, hope, and love. We live in and through the Blessed Sacrament with our Lady of the Blessed Sacrament by our side. Jesus is the center of Mary's life. He is the center of our lives. With Mary, Jesus will be announced to us so that we may share in His agony. With Mary, Jesus will be Baptized in us, so that He may be Resurrected in us from His Eucharistic life into the fullness of the Heavenly Kingdom. With all of these gifts, we will live this side of Heaven in the

---

[103] Mark 14:37, (*New American Bible, revised edition* © (NABRE)).

presence of God. Mary is the Mother of Adorers; she brings us to the Promise of the Father through her Son, Jesus.

St. Peter Julian is familiar with the cross of Christ through his earthly pilgrimage. Mary "drank in long droughts of living waters of grace and love."[104] We will apply ourselves with her consistently to the obedience of our prayers with the same faith, hope, and love that she was graced to receive through her interior life. St. Peter Julian tells us that the sentiments will pass us by, but the truth will remain.[105] "So faith, hope, love remain, these three; but the greatest of these is love" (Corinthians 13:13).

Mary's obedience to the love of God made her perfect. She received God in her body, baptized Him with her love, agonized with Him in His pain, and remained with Him in His Resurrection. We, her loving children, adore Jesus with the Mother of Adorers of the Blessed Sacrament. Living our consecration will be fulfilled by our constancy in prayer and recollection, taking it to the activity rather than the passivity of our lives. Blessed children of God we will be when we live in the Eucharist. St. Peter Julian sends us with this, "The Kingdom of God is within it!"[106]

Take some time to pray about The Kingdom of God living within you.

Daily Prayer: *Veni Creator, Litany of the Most Blessed Sacrament*

---

[104] Eymard, *Our Lady of the Blessed Sacrament*, 149-153.
[105] Ibid.
[106] Ibid.

Mary's Life of Union with Jesus

Mary lived in the Eucharist. He who truly loves, thinks, desires, acts, rejoices or sorrows in the person loved; he is his natural center. Jesus said, " Where thy treasure is, there is thy heart": and to His Apostles: "Abide in Me. Abide in my love, as I abide in my Father's love. "Jesus in the Sacrament lives the same life of love which consumed Him in the days of His mortal existence. In His Sacramental state, he continues to adore His Father by His profound annihilation. He is still the Mediator and Intercessor, before the Divine Goodness, for the salvation of men.

To imitate His obedience, so sweet, so simple and so prompt, she is happy to obey, eager to yield at the least sign. In a word, Mary realizes in herself the Eucharistic life of Jesus Christ. Such ought to be the life of an adorer if he wishes to live in the Eucharist. But to attain this life of union, he must free himself of the slavery of self-love, which seeks self only--even in God's service; which speaks to Jesus of self only, of its own personal affairs; which knows not how to converse with Jesus by speaking to Him of Himself, of the interests of His glory, of the desires of His Sacred Heart.

Jesus has very few adorers who consider themselves sufficiently recompensed and happy in remaining with Him, occupied in serving Him as do the Angels in heaven, as Mary did in the cenacle. He sees at His feet only beggars, or the restless, who seek help. In a royal palace, however, they know their duties as courtiers, know how to wait attendance on the king, seeking only by their presence to honor his majesty. Mary, though, never lost the Eucharistic presence of Jesus. She acted only when He wished it, considering herself well occupied when at His feet, sufficiently recompensed in possessing Him.[107]- St. Peter Julian

St. Peter Julian Eymard has a profound love for the Incarnation, the Word that becomes flesh and lives within us. "Mary realizes in herself the Eucharistic life of Jesus Christ."[108] Mary's consecrated children will find their lives in their own desire for this Eucharistic love and service. This is a gift left to us in God's Promise, in God's Love. In Jesus Eucharistic, we find the intercessor and mediator of the divine goodness for the salvation of the world. We will not only seek him as beggars, but we will serve Him like the Angels in Heaven. Our Blessed Mother was recompensed in possessing Him. Mary, who is the spouse of the Holy Spirit, overshadows us with her love. The inner life of the Trinity allows Mary this joint mission where she realizes the Eucharist in herself. Mary brings us to the Bread of Life, her Son, Jesus, where we will receive the anointing of His Eucharistic life. The Incarnation of God's Love lives on in His children when we become partakers in the divine mystery of the Word made Flesh living within us. This Incarnate life of Jesus Christ projects God's Life within us into the world which He created. The Mother of Adorers was the first to recognize this greatest of Mysteries, Mary's Fiat, her Yes at the Annunciation. She was the first to carry Jesus in her womb; she carried his love. Mary carries us too in finding Jesus' love offered to us in the Blessed Sacrament. We receive Him, and we carry Him in the likeness of our Mother. Jesus again is made Incarnate in us. Jesus' life lives on through us. Of

---

[107] Ibid., 154-158.
[108] Ibid.

ourselves, we are nothing in Him we can do all things. "I have the strength for everything through him who empowers me" (Philippians 4:13).

Pray for a profound love of the Incarnation to abide in us so that we, like Mary, can announce the Holy name of Jesus to the world. Mother of Adorers teach us our life in Jesus Christ Eucharistic, help us abide in a life of union with Him.

Soon we will be reciting our consecration promise to Jesus through Our Lady of the Most Blessed Sacrament. With some final days to prepare, we will continue to reflect on where Mary has taken us. What reflections inspired us in the days of preparation? Take some time to think about the messages that were most prominent in your life, how to apply them to your life, and what they are inspiring you to do. We live out the consecration by keeping the promise as an important reality in our life.

Reflect on one specific grace you have received from the consecration preparation and share it with a friend.

Daily Prayer: Veni Creator, Litany of the Most Blessed Sacrament

CONCLUDING WEEK

THEME: MARY'S TRIUMPH

Intention this week:

Make a perpetual promise to recite a spiritual communion prayer if you cannot get to daily Mass. The faith you place in the prayer is the grace you will receive from it. Continue to journal and prepare for a good and humble confession.

Prayers for each day this week (found in Appendix A)

- Veni Creator
- Litany to the Blessed Virgin Mary

Concluding Week - Day 1

The Perfect Servant of The Blessed Sacrament

"Mary said, "Behold, I am the handmaid of the Lord. May it be done to me according to your word." Then the angel departed from her." (Luke 1:38) Her whole life was passed serving Him in the most perfect manner. She is the perfect model of our Eucharistic service. Her service in the Cenacle sums up her whole life. The spirit of a servant of Jesus is thus defined; devoted love to the Blessed Sacrament in the spirit and virtues of the Blessed Virgin.

Devotedness longs for one thing only, and that is to give pleasure and to fulfill its duty. Our Lord does not ask us to serve Him in the outside world, not even in souls; but He says to us: "To ascend My throne of love, I must have adorers. Without such, I cannot be solemnly exposed. You will be attached to My Person; you will exist for Me, as I shall live for you. You shall go so far as totally to renounce your own will, for I want it for Myself. Renounce your personal interests, I will assume them." A king desires to build up the fortune of his subjects, though he does not tell them what he is going to do. So the field that we have to cultivate is our Lord Himself, Him alone. He retains us for Himself and commits Himself to our care. And the reward of this devotedness? It is to live near the King, to please Him, to be His favorites. Ah, let us serve Him for His own glory and efface ourselves in everything! This devotedness ought, then, to be the devotedness of pure love, pure Eucharistic love for Jesus in the Blessed Sacrament. This love should absorb all else to become associated with the Eucharist! To become one of the staff of Jesus Christ! What is there greater on earth or in heaven? Love flies; it loves the service of Jesus better than its own repose, its own gratification. When we do not love, we do not want to go too fast, we delay our steps. But, like Mary, let us fly to the service of adoration of Jesus in the Eucharist who is waiting for us.

The service of our Lord is, therefore, a duty for us as it was for Mary. You are called to serve Him and not yourself. Let us be true servants of the Blessed Sacrament, as Mary was; servants who have no longer any other interests, no longer any personality, who are entirely consumed in the service of Jesus. What a beautiful title is this-the "handmaid," the servant of the Lord. It is the only one that she gave herself. Ah if anyone should be humble and devoted it is the servant of the Lord! Adoration is the sum total of her whole life. Therefore, to serve Jesus in the Most Blessed Sacrament, after the example of our Lady of the Cenacle, and as she did- there is the life of the true servant. His motto is: "All for the service of Jesus Eucharistic, in union with Mary!"[109]- St. Peter Julian

"Love flies; it loves the service of Jesus better than its own repose, its own gratification."[110] St. Peter Julian is surely expressing his own life in the Eucharist here as he expresses love for Our Lady. Make your life a living prayer. This will be our lives after our consecration promise. Everything we do should be silently entwined in our union with Jesus in the Blessed Sacrament through Mary. Our Lady is the handmaid of the Lord, for she served Jesus perfectly. She adores him from

[109] Ibid., 159-164.
[110] Ibid.

the womb to His glorified life, and still adores Him with us in His Eucharistic life. When we ask Mary to clothe us in the virtues of her love we are asking her to clothe us in the hidden life of Jesus Eucharistic. Mary is the perfect servant of the Blessed Sacrament. Why? Because Mary worships her son, she adores God. St. Peter Julian sees this in Mary, "Renounce your personal interests, I will assume them." [111] The scriptures confirm St. Peter Julian's word through Isaiah, "The Light of Israel will become a fire, the Holy One, a flame, That burns and consumes its briers and its thorns in a single day" (Isaiah 6:17). Mary's graces are multiplied. She is inviting us to trust in the fact that all we need will be given to us and so much more when we serve Jesus Eucharistic. The grace-filled strength this lowly handmaid encompasses in her soul can only come from the grace of God. Mary is the perfect servant, for after her worship, she cares for her children, you and me. This is her daily duty. St. Peter Julian tells us we need to be attached to Jesus' person in the Blessed Sacrament. The grace we need to carry out our own daily duties, whatever they may be, needs to flow from our life in the Eucharistic Lord through the heart of our Mother. St. Peter Julian tells us we need not serve the world. Our devotion needs to be serving Jesus Eucharistic. Our service will then take flight through His love and fly!

When we enter into the mystery of God's love more deeply St. Peter Julian reminds us that we will not know where He will take us. "Though he does not tell them what he is going to do."[112] Jesus simply asks us to be devoted. His life in us will then manifest in all we do; "To become associated with the Eucharist! to become one of the staff of Jesus Christ! What is

---

[111] Ibid.
[112] Ibid.

there greater on earth or in heaven?"[113] We will serve Jesus most perfectly when we serve Him with Mary. Children who love their mom want to emulate her, to be like her for all that she gives. We who are Mary's children must meditate on her heart, emulate the love that comes from it, and give back for all that she sacrifices. We do not know where He will take us, nor do we know the hour or moment in which He will come to us. "Therefore, stay awake, for you know neither the day nor the hour" (Matthew 25:13). But we do know He has prepared a place for us; " And whatever you ask in my name, I will do, so that the Father may be glorified in the Son" (John 14:13). Mary, help us to love. Lead us to be perfect servants of the Blessed Sacrament. Help us to enter into the mystery of God's love.

Jesus wants us to adore Him because He loves us so much. Our time with Him is our only way to salvation. Jesus knows we need the graces that flow from his Eucharistic Heart. Take this grace from His Eucharistic Heart and apply it to your own life. Pray when you are before the Blessed Sacrament. St. Peter Julian suggests letting your prayer flow from adoring, to thanksgiving, to forgiveness, to intercession. Ask how to love Jesus more. Pray deeply for the duties your life is calling you to and how you can bring your Eucharistic love into your day by never separating from the presence of God within you. St. Peter Julian tells us that, "Adoration is the sum total of her whole life."[114] If Adoration is the sum of Mary's whole life, this means adoration never left her. Mary brought adoration into her whole life. This is how life becomes a living prayer. We have been given an invitation to make a fervent spiritual

---

[113] Ibid.
[114] Ibid.

Communion if we cannot attend daily Mass. This practice is an entrance into a life of adoration of the Blessed Sacrament. If your state in life does not offer you even a small opportunity to sit before the Eucharist, sit at home. Make your home a house of prayer. It may cost you some sleep but rise and pray. Make a holy hour at home, or a holy half hour or even twenty minutes. Set a routine and follow it as best as you can. Never despair if your day does not allow you time, just begin again. God may be calling you to care for your children or loved ones. If this is His Will, be at peace and remember we only strive to offer prayer. The call to build Eucharistic communities is essential for the restoration of all that is lost. The consecration promise is the handing over of our will to the will of God. If we long to be with Jesus in the Blessed Sacrament, He will find a way for us to be with him. We do need to persevere in this desire for holiness. It is our choice, a choice that will be blessed by His grace. St. Peter Julian sums it up himself with these most important words, "All for the service of Jesus Eucharistic, in union with Mary!"[115]

Pray today on all that your daily duties ask of you, on how you can add more prayer time, and on what you will need to give up in order to offer that time to Jesus.

Daily Prayer: Veni Creator, Litany to the Blessed Virgin Mary

---

[115] Ibid., 163.

Mary's Triumph

On the day of her glorious Assumption into heaven, Mary received the crown of all her graces. Truly we should rejoice, for, although our Mother has been taken from us, we have not lost her. We simply send her before us to prepare our place in heaven and acquire for us certain rights over the Heart of God. The triumph of Mary is also the triumph of Jesus. Jesus loved his mother so much, Mary died of love; the longing to see her Son and to be re-united with Him snapped her thread of life. Jesus is now to accord her a grand triumph.

Jesus himself introduces His Mother to the glorified state; He owes her compensation. She enters by a special gate, open for her alone. If the twelve Apostles are the twelve gates of heaven, Mary is the royal entrance to that celestial country, the gate par excellence. O august and holy Gate! Jesus leads His Mother by the hand, up to the very Throne of God: "Behold, O Father, her with whom Thou art associated by Thy choice of her as My Mother-to give me my humanity!" And the Father therewith crowns her with her three most beautiful titles: Queen, Mother, and Mediatrix. But in Mary's diadem, there are three pearls that shine with an even more dazzling brightness-the pearls of her humility, of her poverty, and of her suffering. Mary was the most humble of all creatures, consequently, in heaven, she is now the most glorious.

The demon has been forced to acknowledge that he is never sure of victory so long as he whom Mary protects retains a breath of life. She supplicates, importunes and snatches, as it were, from

God the graces of mercy and pardon for the most hardened
sinners. It was God's Will that Mary should suffer a continual
martyrdom. Simeon's prophecy poisoned all her joy. From the
moment of its utterance, Mary substituted for Jesus while He
was still too young to suffer publicly. In a word, God has
crowned Mary with glory and honor as the Masterpiece of His
love. He alone is greater than she: "Solo tonante minor!" But, in
the midst of her glory, Mary never forgets that she is our Mother.
She ascended to heaven before us to facilitate our entrance there
and to conduct us thither. She herself will come for us at that
supreme moment of our lives- the hour of our death- if we only
summon to her aid![116]- St. Peter Julian

Mary's Triumph! St. Peter Julian Eymard can attest to
these words in his founding of the Congregation of the Blessed
Sacrament. The Congregation currently blesses the Catholic
Church with priests, brothers, sister servants and lay aggregates
throughout the world. St. Peter Julian knew precisely what
Mary's triumph would offer those who love her, "The Triumph
of Mary is also the triumph of Jesus."[117] Our Blessed Mother
has only one desire, and that is to bring us closer to Jesus
Christ truly present in the Blessed Sacrament. Mary's hope
would be for the Consecration Preparation to inspire us to
make holy hours before the Blessed Sacrament a weekly prayer
routine. Mary has taken us somewhere through the life of St.
Peter Julian Eymard. In our time of preparation, we have made
a promise to remain close to Mary so that she may guide our
lives as the good mother she is into the heart of Jesus Christ.
When Jesus triumphs in our lives, Mary is triumphant.

---

[116] Ibid., 165-171.
[117] Ibid.

"Mary died of love; the longing to see her Son and to be re-united with Him snapped her thread of life." [118] This statement by St. Peter Julian is so powerful. We hear in it detachment from the things of this world, not detachment from love, but to the things of this world. Mary "snapped" her thread of life. May our consecration promise give us a glimpse into this kind of love for God, so that we will strive through this earthly pilgrimage to snap out of this life into Heaven. This is Mary's grand triumph! St. Peter Julian continues to give us this visual to desire holiness, "If the twelve Apostles are the twelve gates of heaven."[119] The twelve give their lives in testimony to the life in Jesus Christ. This is the mission of the church from the beginning and our continued mission as consecrated children of Mary. The Apostles, by the twelve gates, make their entrance way into the divine light of Heaven, where Mary is the "gate par excellence."[120] This seems like an invitation into the gate of Heaven by the Heart of our Mother. Mary guides us through this life and carries us into eternity by her way of love. St. Peter Julian offers us this thought that inspires us to cling to our good Mother, "The demon has been forced to acknowledge that he is never sure of victory so long as he whom Mary protects retains a breath."[121] Jesus assures us, "And whatever you ask in my name, I will do, so that the Father may be glorified in the Son" (John 14:30). The darkness has no power over the light. God's Triumph comes to us in following His Son, Jesus Christ, who is truly present in the Blessed Sacrament. God's triumph comes to us in the gift of the Lady

---

[118] Ibid.
[119] Ibid.
[120] Ibid.
[121] Ibid.

of Light, who will keep us free from all that will try to darken our hearts. We should cling to Mary. We who will consecrate our lives through Her, will be reunited with Jesus in the fullness of His eternal glory. St. Peter Julian confirms this thought, "Mary never forgets that she is our Mother. She ascended to Heaven before us to facilitate our entrance there and to conduct us thither. She herself will come for us at that supreme moment of our lives- the hour of our death- if we only summon to her aid!"[122] Mother keep us close to you!

Time to prepare. Our preparation continues throughout this week until the day of our Consecration. Mary's triumph will live through her consecrated children, we who keep Jesus Eucharistic alive and well and with us through the testimonies of our lives. We live our faith by the example of God's love made manifest through us. We cannot give Whom we do not have. We need to keep our love for Holy Communion at the center of our lives by the sacramental or spiritual reception of Jesus. The Consecration Promise too must be kept alive, not filed or set aside for next time, but renewed with hope daily. It would be suggested to add a prayer to your day so that you can recall what we have done throughout these preparation days. You may simply take on the prayer to Our Lady of the Blessed Sacrament or the Daily Promise. By this offering, you will keep the relationship that you have formed well nourished. The consecration promise will be as real to your heart as you keep it. We will be consecrated to Our Lady of the Most Blessed Sacrament. What greater gift can we receive? And we will still receive more in Jesus Eucharistic. St. Peter Julian concludes with this thought, "In a word, God has crowned Mary with

---

[122] Ibid.

glory and honor as the Masterpiece of His love. He alone is greater than she: "Solo tonante minor!"'[123] Mary's triumph of love continues through our consecrated lives of love to Jesus through her. The Promise of the Father will shine through us by Mary.

"He will wipe every tear from their eyes, and there shall be no more death or mourning, wailing or pain, [for] the old order has passed away" (Revelation 21:4).

The triumph of Mary is also the triumph of Jesus. St. Peter Julian Eymard, Apostle of the Eucharist, pray for us.

If you are able, recite the Litany of the Blessed Virgin Mary aloud. Ponder which verse is most prominent to you right now and pray on what Our Lady may be calling you to do.

Daily Prayer: Veni Creator, Litany to the Blessed Virgin Mary

---

[123] Ibid.

Mary's Pearl of Humility

In the last three days before the recitation of our promise, we will look at the pearls of Mary's Crown from the heart of St. Peter Julian Eymard.

Jesus himself introduces His Mother to the glorified state; He owes her compensation. She enters by a special gate, open for her alone. If the twelve Apostles are the twelve gates of heaven, Mary is the royal entrance to that celestial country, the gate par excellence. O august and holy Gate! Jesus leads His Mother by the hand, up to the very Throne of God: "Behold, O Father, her with whom Thou art associated by Thy choice of her as My Mother-to give me my humanity!" And the Father therewith crowns her with her three most beautiful titles: Queen, Mother, and Mediatrix. But in Mary's diadem, there are three pearls that shine with an even more dazzling brightness-the pearls of her humility, of her poverty, and of her suffering. – St. Peter Julian

---

St. Peter Julian Eymard reminds us that the spirit of God descended upon Our Lady. We will see Mary with ever greater light as we look at the pearl of her humility. This pearl of Mary's Crown will radiate her love unto us, her children. Our Lady has had a great place in our Consecration Preparation. She will keep us in the divine light. We need to keep close to her maternal care. The Catechism teaches us that, "Our moral life has its source in faith in God who reveals his love to us" (CCC 2087). Mary had full confidence in God's Love. Her faith

143

is the faith she longs for us to have. Mary was entrusted with the heavenly Father's Son. She entered into the mystery of God's love by an interior movement of the natural love written on her heart. The total submission of Mary's will is offered to the creator of her soul. The moral life, the life of God's goodness, was recognized by Mary. She sensed God was all good and deserving of our love. St. Peter Julian considers Mary as Queen, to be one of her most beautiful titles. Mary is Queen for she is the mother of the royal family, God's family. Jesus is King and Mary is the Queen who stands at the Gate of Heaven, the entrance to the supremacy of our lives. The Holy Spirit, the spirit of truth and holiness, overshadowed Our Lady with the divine power. Mary handed over Her will to the glory of God and became the handmaid of her Lord by her yes. Humble submission to God could only come from Mary's faith in the Father. Our Lady knew by this faith that empowered her heart that there was another place other than this world- the world of God which her heart entered by its connection to the favor she knew was upon her. Our Blessed Mother trusted in God as her Father. Her faith came from her humility, offered through trust, and she was presented with the title of Queen. This is Mary's triumph, her humility.

Our Lady of the Most Blessed Sacrament's pearl of humility, a diadem in her crown, granted her the title of Queen. Queen Mary greatest of all in faith in the Holy Trinity, chosen for us in the Promise of Our Father, pray for us your consecrated children.

Ponder and pray on the faith of Our Blessed Mother, her entrance into the mystery of salvation and her humility.

Daily Prayer: Veni Creator, Litany to the Blessed Virgin Mary

Concluding Week - Day 4

Mary's Pearl of Poverty

Jesus himself introduces His Mother to the glorified state; He owes her compensation. She enters by a special gate, open for her alone. If the twelve Apostles are the twelve gates of heaven, Mary is the royal entrance to that celestial country, the gate par excellence. O august and holy Gate! Jesus leads His Mother by the hand, up to the very Throne of God: "Behold, O Father, her with whom Thou art associated by Thy choice of her as My Mother to give me my humanity!" And the Father therewith crowns her with her three most beautiful titles: Queen, Mother, and Mediatrix. But in Mary's diadem there are three pearls that shine with an even more dazzling brightness the pearls of her humility, of her poverty, and of her suffering. – St. Peter Julian

St. Peter Julian tells us of the second pearl that shines in Mary's royal diadem, her poverty. This pearl of poverty is her hope in the Son of God who takes away the sins of the world. Jesus' life incarnated in the womb of the Blessed Virgin Mary gains her the "three most beautiful titles." The title, Mother, is the one that Mary deems most sacred. Our Lady's motherhood was a natural gift that she could offer back to God the Father for she was conceived without original sin, pure, and undefiled. The life within her made Mary proclaim the greatness of the Lord. She was keenly aware that the life within her was precious. The Catechism tells us that, "Hope is the theological virtue by which we desire the Kingdom of Heaven and eternal life as our happiness, placing our trust in Christ's promises and relying not on our own strength, but on the help of the grace of the Holy Spirit" (CCC 1817). Mary's hope was in God's life within her, where God's Grace, God's Love, and God's Power was found. Mary's happiness was found in her Son's promise for our redemption and the overshadowing of the Holy Spirit. This overshadowing preserved her in hope. Mary recognized the divine power over her. Her hope would be to hold the "royal entrance" as Mother for her children, who she loves from the Eucharistic Kingdom, into the fullness of Eternity. Mary's motherhood gave her hope for the whole world in her Son. St. Peter Julian adds, "...as my Mother to give me my humanity!"[124] Mary restored the dignity of our humanity by joyfully bringing the Son of God into the world in poverty. Jesus born in a stable was everything to Mary. Our Lady of the Most Blessed Sacrament's greatest poverty was that of her spirit. Mary was poor in spirit. Chosen from God's love, this love dwelled within Her own heart. She lives in the heart of the children of God. Mary loses herself to gain their love. She is Mother most merciful by her poor spirit. Her title of Mother, her love for her Son, and Mary's hope in all that the Promise of the Father gave her, allowed her to give everything to us. The triumph of Mary is the Triumph of Jesus!

Our Lady of the Most Blessed Sacrament's pearl of poverty, a pearl in her crown, granted her the title of Mother. Mother Mary, chosen for us in the Promise of Our Father, pray for us your consecrated children. Ponder and pray on the hope of Our Blessed Mother, her entrance into the mystery of salvation and the poverty she lovingly accepted.

Daily Prayer: Veni Creator, Litany to the Blessed Virgin Mary

---

[124] Ibid.

Concluding Week - Day 5

Mary's Pearl of Suffering

Jesus himself introduces His Mother to the glorified state; He owes her compensation. She enters by a special gate, open for her alone. If the twelve Apostles are the twelve gates of heaven, Mary is the royal entrance to that celestial country, the gate par excellence. O august and holy Gate! Jesus leads His Mother by the hand, up to the very Throne of God: "Behold, O Father, her with whom Thou art associated by Thy choice of her as My Mother-to give me my humanity!" And the Father therewith crowns her with her three most beautiful titles: Queen, Mother, and Mediatrix. But in Mary's diadem, there are three pearls that shine with an even more dazzling brightness-the pearls of her humility, of her poverty, and of her suffering. – St. Peter Julian

---

St. Peter Julian Eymard recognized his life in the Eucharist, lived his life in the Eucharist, and calls down from Heaven to the children of God to find their life in the Eucharist, Jesus truly present in the Blessed Sacrament. Tomorrow is the day of our Consecration to Our Lady of the Most Blessed Sacrament. We promise Mary that we will adore her Son. We live in the family of God by our Baptism and nurture this family life by the dedication of our love within it. Today we will take a final look from the heart of St. Peter Julian at the "three most beautiful titles." Mediatrix will be a grand way to close our preparation and then open a life of servitude to our Eucharistic King through the heart of Mary. Mary is Mediatrix of all grace. She will be our intercessor of God's power, His Love, and His life within us.

Our Lady, who is Mediatrix, is empowered by the crown of God's gifts in the pearl of suffering. St. Peter Julian tells us that,

> Simeon's prophecy poisoned all her joy. From the moment of its utterance, Mary substituted for Jesus while He was still too young to suffer publicly. And at the foot of the cross she is nearest to Jesus in order that she may suffer more. Because Jesus wished to have her nearest to Him in heaven, He united her more than any other creature to His sufferings and humiliations while on earth. In a word, God has crowned Mary with glory and honor as the Masterpiece of His love.[125]

The words, "Mary substituted" should console our hearts as we have this Mediatrix of Grace to stand with us in the poison of sufferings, the hardships of life, the crosses, toils, and disappointments that we will endure. We need not ever be alone. Mary is our Mediatrix of Joy who rejoices with us in the gift of the Word made flesh in our own lives. Mary's love is offered to us. She shares in our sufferings, they become her sufferings. She shares in our joys, they become her joys. Mary is our Mediatrix and Our Lady of the Most Blessed Sacrament. She will carry us as she carried Jesus. Mary lived in the "greatest of these"[126], love. Mary longs for her children to live in the love of God the Father. Mary's spousal love for the Holy Spirit is the perfection of God living in her. The gifts of the Holy Spirit flow from her existence. Mary is Mediatrix of love by the way of her suffering. Our Lady's suffering is the outpour of Her life for us. She gives the "Gift of herself" to God. She

---

[125] Ibid., 168.
[126] 1 Corinthians 13:13.

lives in His Will, in His Love. Mary's triumph is the triumph of Jesus! Jesus' life is manifested through her. Mary offers to us, her loving consecrated children, this same manifestation by uniting very closely to Jesus Eucharistic. Mary, Mediatrix, who is Our Lady of the Blessed Sacrament, guide our lives after our Consecration Promise to call on you as Queen, Mother and Mediatrix by your royal crown. Our Lady of the Blessed Sacrament carry us as you carried your Son into the world through God's love.

Mary, Mediatrix of all grace we pray for your intentions to become our own for the salvation of all your children.

Our Lady of the Blessed Sacrament's pearl of suffering in her crown, granted her the title Mediatrix. Mary, Mediatrix of God's love by the power of the Holy Spirit, keep us in the fullness of the gifts of the spirit so we too may receive the Promise of Our Father. Our Lady of the Most Blessed Sacrament pray for us your consecrated children.

Ponder and pray for the hope Our Blessed Mother had, for the same entrance into the mystery of salvation and the suffering she lovingly accepted.

Daily Prayer: Veni Creator, Litany to the Blessed Virgin Mary

Saint Peter Julian Eymard

ACT OF CONSECRATION

*M*other of the Word of God, you offer to us your Son living in the Eucharist. Our Lady of the Most Blessed Sacrament, you feed us with the fruit of your womb, Jesus. In the light of the Holy Spirit you illumine our hearts with Holy Wisdom.

I admire the excellence of your adoration and Eucharistic service in the Cenacle. I now give myself entirely to you to guard and direct my vocation as an adorer. I place into your hands the direction of my vocation and the graces of the awesome duties that it asks of me. My vocation of adorer is the most beautiful of all, since it retains me forever in the service of the Person of Jesus Christ in His Divine Sacrament. Into your hands I place the direction of my vocation and the graces of the sublime duties it asks of me. My vocation of adorer is beautiful, the most beautiful of all, since it keeps me forever in the service of the Adorable Person of Jesus Christ in His Divine Sacrament.

My vocation is awe-inspiring; to share the service of the angels and, dare I say, of the Blessed Virgin herself, in the praise of Jesus. For this vocation, I should have some true virtues, and, at least, ordinary piety —but, alas! I have nothing, and I am nothing! I can do nothing! You chose me, poor infirm creature, a nothing full of miseries, still covered with the scars of my sins, still with the old self that lives in me. How dare I accept this grace, to be in the same house with your Holy Mother, to remain in your company and in your presence?

0 Mary, my celestial Queen and my Divine Mother, I can only accept the honor of becoming the happy servant of our Eucharistic Jesus, if you consent to form me, to raise me, and to clothe me with your spirit, your virtues, your merits. Take me for your child, Queen and Mother of the servants of Jesus. You who love only in Jesus and for Jesus! I place into your hands, my good Mother, the grace and the

151

service of my vocation. I give myself to you, in return give Jesus to me. Formed and presented by you, O good Mother, Jesus, my sweet Master, will receive me kindly and love me in you.

My vocation is beautiful; its duties are great and holy. I desire to spend my life in adoration at the foot of Incarnate Love. Before that Eucharistic throne, I will join the angels and saints in what they do and will eternally do in heaven: praising the infinite bounty of God and blessing the boundless mercy of God. With this gift-of-self, I devote my life to live the mystery of the Eucharist fully and make known the love of God in service to others.

I desire to live with Jesus in the Host, like the Blessed Virgin at Nazareth and in the Cenacle, like the saints in glory, united in love and care of others. My mission is that of Magdalen, contemplative, with the Queen of the Apostles in the Cenacle, praying before the tabernacle, converting the world by her prayer at the foot of the Eucharist; that of St. Teresa, St. Catherine of Siena, and of all those holy souls who carry on a continuous apostolate of prayer and self-offering. I ought to honor in an entirely special manner the interior and hidden life of Jesus in the Blessed Sacrament.

O my good Mother, since you agree to become my teacher, you will let me adore Jesus with you, bless Jesus with your praises, entreat Jesus with your prayers, serve Jesus with your hands, love Jesus with your heart, glorify Jesus with your sanctity. I will be your disciple, your child, and, shall I say it? —a little Mary, another you, —the servant of Jesus! I shall tell you simply and honestly my faults, O my good Mother! I shall give you the tiny flowers of virtue that I have gathered, and you will offer all to Jesus, with myself along with yourself. On this condition alone, I hope to become a true servant of the Most Blessed Sacrament. My God, behold your humble servant! Let it be done to me according to your merciful goodness and your grace of love! Our Lady of the Most Blessed Sacrament, Mother and Model of Adorers, pray for us who have recourse to thee![127]

---

[127] Promise text adapted by Rev. William Fickel, SSS - 5/13/17.

THE ETERNAL PROMISE

Consecration as a Lifelong Dedication

- Continue to set ten minutes aside each day to pray.
- Renew the promise daily through the suggested short Daily Promise found in Appendix A.
- Attend daily Mass if possible or recite the spiritual communion prayer.
- Try to find time for Adoration of the Blessed Sacrament, if you are able, make a commitment to sign up for an hour.
- Pray the Liturgy of the Hours if you are able, especially morning and evening prayer.
- Pray the Holy Rosary daily, allowing the virtues connected to the life of Christ guide you in your journey of faith.
- Make Marian feast days special by reciting the consecration promise as a renewal.
- Make your life a living prayer by taking the contemplative union of your life into the service you are called to daily.
- Renew your consecration annually by preparing as if it was the first time. You may reread this book annually forever or take on another spiritual

exercise. However, begin and conclude on the same day each year with the recitation of your promise as a zealous offering to God.

St. Peter Julian Eymard tells us:

Our Lord has prepared us a long time. He has hedged us about with graces from our infancy, in order to introduce us into the Cenacle of His Eucharist. Let us thank Him with all our heart. Although we may not have given ourselves to Him at so early an age as Mary, we are, however, still in the beginning of the Eucharistic life. The Eucharistic manifestation has only just begun, and our Lord calls us to be among the first to work for its development.[128]

We are called to serve, first and foremost through our prayers as adorers of the Blessed Sacrament. We need to build our Eucharistic communities of love directing our hearts to the living God. Our Father will balance our life of prayer and work; however we do need to pray. May Mary's life of union with Jesus be given to her beloved children.

God's Promise never ends, it is ETERNAL! With grateful hearts we have consecrated our lives to Jesus through our Lady of the Most Blessed Sacrament through the charism of St. Peter Julian Eymard. Our lives are now offered as a perpetual gift of self through our sacrificial love given to Our Heavenly Father. Where do we go from here? St. Peter Julian directs our souls in these words: *"THE EUCHARISTIC MANIFESTATION HAS ONLY JUST BEGUN!"*

---

[128] Eymard, *Our Lady of the Blessed Sacrament*, 33-37.

AFTERWORD

*"He who consecrates and those who are being consecrated all have
one origin." (Hebrews 2:11)*

One may wonder how this 33-day method of preparation
to consecrate your life to Jesus through Our Lady of the Most
Blessed Sacrament came into existence.

In 1999 I consecrated my life to Jesus through Mary for
the first time, and my life was forever changed. The intimate
relationship that I formed with Mary remains a significant part
of my spiritual life. This relationship was nourished as I
prepared each year to renew my consecration promise. This
was an extraordinary time of grace, which culminated with the
formal recitation of the promise annually, on March 25th, the
Solemnity of the Annunciation of the Lord.

At the time of my first consecration I lived in New York
where there was a group of ladies who shared the consecration
journey with me. We have genuinely remained spiritual sisters
in Christ. When my family moved to Florida, I kept the
devotion each year, beginning my preparation on the 20th of
February to conclude my consecration on March 25th. I would
recite my consecration promise in front of the Tabernacle, by
myself, for ten years. When my family became part of a home

school community, I extended an email inviting the moms to join in the consecration. It was well received, and we have a wonderful group now participating together. Each year we used a different consecration method[129], one better than the next. Consecration Day became a lovely day to look forward to. We had flowers, cake, and a celebration after the recitation of the promise, all following Holy Mass. In 2017, through prayer, the Holy Spirit guided me to use St. Peter Julian Eymard's Library Vol. 7, *Our Lady of the Blessed Sacrament*, for our consecration preparation.

The Eymard library (containing nine books) has been a significant part of my life for the past twenty years; the books became a perpetual evening read for me. St. Peter Julian, the favored Saint of my heart, gives direction and beauty to the soul by embracing the treasure of grace he has left the Catholic Church in his spirituality and writings. After sharing with the ladies (and men) that we would be using the Eymard Library (Volume 7) to consecrate, the journey began.

Ivonne Hernandez, in tune to the Holy Spirit, suggested we share the consecration journey through an online blog. We prayed about what we should name this blog. The phrase "The Promise of the Father" came to me clearly when I prayed the *Veni Creator,* one of my morning offerings. Ivonne pointed out it is the meaning of the name Elizabeth, or Elisheba, in its Hebrew form. We had our name, Elisheba Blog.[130] Ivonne asked me to lead the 33-day preparation to Our Lady of the Blessed Sacrament by posting daily reflections on St. Peter Julian's writings. With all of the thoughts that flashed by, I was praying to Jesus through Mary, at daily Mass, and somehow, I

---

[129] There are different books or "methods" to consecrate oneself.
[130] www.elishebahouse.com/blog.

knew clearly in my soul I was supposed to form this method of preparation. There is no education, nothing in this life more excellent than finding Jesus in the Most Blessed Sacrament and keeping the love and friendship with Him alive. Mary, our good Mother, has always been part of my life. Praying the scriptures through the Holy Rosary, just as Mary promised, sent signal graces that etched my heart, and I am a forever grateful daughter of Mary.

My daily Mass intention was offered for the work, specifically asking for the power of the Holy Spirit, along with Mary, to project the words Jesus would want to come forth through me. I was blessed to have Father William Fickel's guidance and support throughout the days of writing. The homilies offered at daily Mass were the inspiration that helped form this spiritual exercise.

I am forever grateful to Our Lady for leading us to this consecration to Jesus through her title, OUR LADY OF THE MOST BLESSED SACRAMENT. St. Peter Julian Eymard will bless you with his love for Our Blessed Mother. Our Lady guided him to form the Congregation of the Blessed Sacrament. The work of Jesus Eucharistic was made manifest in his life, and his life was complete in the Lord this side of Heaven. With the guidance of St. Peter Julian Eymard through the Heart of Mary, may this method to prepare to consecrate your life to Jesus through Our Lady of the Most Blessed Sacrament forever keep you in the presence of GOD!

"Do thou be their Mother, O thou strong one."[131] Mary!

---

[131] Eymard, *Our Lady of the Blessed Sacrament*, 95.

May the ROLA/Rule of Life for Associates of the Blessed Sacrament inspire you to live in the Eucharistic Heart of Jesus through Mary:

> The Virgin Mary, the Mother of Jesus and of the Church, is the indispensable model of the Eucharistic life. She shared the disciples' life of prayer in the Cenacle and their apostolic journeying in the world.

> Like her, we let ourselves be guided by the Spirit so that, docile to his action, we may contribute effectively to the coming of the Kingdom.

> We honor and also invoke her by the title:

> *"Our Lady of the Blessed Sacrament."*[132]

---

[132] ROLA #11.

APPENDIX A: PRAYERS

Prayers

Spiritual Communion

My Jesus, I believe that you are present in
the most Holy Sacrament.
I love you above all things and I desire to
receive You into my soul.
Since I cannot now receive You sacramentally,
come at least spiritually into my heart.
I unite myself wholly to You;
never permit me to be separated from You.

Daily Promise

My vocation is beautiful; its duties are great and holy. I desire to
spend my life in adoration at the foot of Incarnate Love. Before
that Eucharistic throne, I will join the angels and saints in what
they do and will eternally do in heaven: praising the infinite
bounty of God and blessing the boundless mercy of God. With
this gift-of-self, I devote my life to live the mystery of the
Eucharist fully and make known the love of God in service to
others.

Our Lady of the Blessed Sacrament

Blessed are you, Mary exalted daughter of Sion!
You are highly favoured and full of grace,
for the spirit of God descended upon you.
We magnify the Lord and rejoice with you for the gift of the Word
made flesh, bread of life and cup of joy.

Our Lady of the Blessed Sacrament,
our model of prayer in the Cenacle,
pray for us that we may become what we receive,
the body of Christ your son. Amen.

Veni Creator

Come, O Creator Spirit blest,
And in our souls take up Thy rest,
Come with Thy grace and Heavenly aid,
To fill the hearts which Thou hast made.

Great Paraclete! To Thee we cry,
O highest gift of God most high!
O fount of life! O fire of love!
And sweet anointing from above.

Thou in Thy sevenfold gifts art known,
The finger of God's hand we own;
The promise of the Father, Thou!
Who dost the tongue with power endow.

Kindle our senses from above,
And make our hearts over flow with love;
With patience firm and virtues high,
The weakness of our flesh supply.

Far from us drive the foe we dread,
And grant us Thy true peace instead;
So shall we not, with Thee for guide,
Turn from the path of life aside.

And, may Thy grace on us bestow
The Father and the Son to know,
And Thee through endless times confessed
Of both the Eternal Spirit blest.

All glory while the ages run
Be to the Father and the Son
Who rose from death; the same to Thee,
O Holy Spirit, eternally. Amen

Ave Maris Stella

Hail bright star of ocean,
God's own Mother blest,
Ever sinless Virgin,
Gate of heavenly rest.

Taking that sweet Ave,
Which from Gabriel came,
Peace confirm within us,
Changing Eva's name.

Break the captives' fetters,
Light on blindness pour,
All our ills expelling,
Every bliss implore.

Show thyself a Mother;
May the Word Divine,
Born for us thy Infant,
Hear our prayers through thine.

Virgin all excelling,
Mildest of the mild,
Freed from guilt, preserve us,
Pure and undefiled.

Keep our life all spotless,
Make our way secure,
Till we find in Jesus,
Joy forevermore.

Through the highest heaven
To the Almighty Three,
Father, Son and Spirit,
One same glory be.
Amen.

Litany of the Holy Spirit

Lord, *have mercy on us.*
Christ, *have mercy on us.*
Lord, *have mercy on us.*

Father all powerful, *have mercy on us.*
Jesus, Eternal Son of the Father, Redeemer of the world, *save us.*
Spirit of the Father and the Son, boundless life of both, *sanctify us.*
Holy Trinity, *hear us.*

Holy Spirit, Who proceedest from the Father and the Son,
enter our hearts.
Holy Spirit, Who art equal to the Father and the Son,
enter our hearts.

Promise of God the Father, *have mercy on us.*
Ray of heavenly light, *have mercy on us.*
Author of all good, *have mercy on us.*
Source of heavenly water, *have mercy on us.*
Consuming fire, *have mercy on us.*
Ardent charity, *have mercy on us.*
Spiritual unction, *have mercy on us.*
Spirit of love and truth, *have mercy on us.*
Spirit of wisdom and understanding, *have mercy on us.*
Spirit of counsel and fortitude, *have mercy on us.*
Spirit of knowledge and piety, *have mercy on us.*
Spirit of the fear of the Lord, *have mercy on us.*
Spirit of grace and prayer, *have mercy on us.*
Spirit of peace and meekness, *have mercy on us.*
Spirit of modesty and innocence, *have mercy on us.*
Holy Spirit, the Comforter, *have mercy on us.*
Holy Spirit, the Sanctifier, *have mercy on us.*
Holy Spirit, Who governest the Church, *have mercy on us.*
Gift of God, the Most High, *have mercy on us.*
Spirit Who fillest the universe, *have mercy on us.*
Spirit of the adoption of the children of God, *have mercy on us.*

Holy Spirit, *inspire us with the horror of sin.*
Holy Spirit, *come and renew the face of the earth.*
Holy Spirit, *shed Thy light in our souls.*
Holy Spirit, *engrave Thy law in our hearts.*
Holy Spirit, *inflame us with the flame of Thy love.*
Holy Spirit, *open to us the treasures of Thy graces.*
Holy Spirit, *teach us to pray well.*
Holy Spirit, *enlighten us with Thy heavenly inspirations.*
Holy Spirit, *lead us in the way of salvation.*
Holy Spirit, *grant us the only necessary knowledge.*
Holy Spirit, *inspire in us the practice of good.*
Holy Spirit, *grant us the merits of all virtues.*
Holy Spirit, *make us persevere in justice.*
Holy Spirit, *be Thou our everlasting reward.*

Lamb of God, Who takest away the sins of the world, *send us Thy Holy Spirit.*
Lamb of God, Who takest away the sins of the world, *pour down into our souls the gifts of the Holy Spirit.*
Lamb of God, Who takest away the sins of the world, *grant us the Spirit of wisdom and piety.*
Come, Holy Spirit! Fill the hearts of Thy faithful.
And enkindle in them the fire of Thy love.

Let us Pray
Grant, O merciful Father, that Thy Divine Spirit enlighten, inflame and purify us, that He may penetrate us with His heavenly dew and make us fruitful in good works; through our Lord Jesus Christ, Thy Son, Who with Thee, in the unity of the same Spirit, liveth and reigneth forever and ever. Amen.

Litany of the Most Blessed Sacrament

Lord, have mercy. R. *Lord, have mercy.*
Christ, have mercy. R. *Christ, have mercy.*
Lord, have mercy. R. *Lord, have mercy.*
Christ, hear us. R. *Christ, graciously hear us.*
God the Father of Heaven, R. *have mercy on us.*
God the Son, Redeemer of the world, R. *have mercy on us.*
God the Holy Spirit, R. *have mercy on us.*
Holy Trinity, one God, R. *have mercy on us.*

Jesus, Eternal High Priest of the Eucharistic Sacrifice,
R. *have mercy on us.*
Jesus, Divine Victim on the Altar for our salvation,
R. *have mercy on us.*
Jesus, hidden under the appearance of bread,
R. *have mercy on us.*
Jesus, dwelling in the tabernacles of the world,
R. *have mercy on us.*
Jesus, really, truly and substantially present in the Blessed
Sacrament, R. *have mercy on us.*
Jesus, abiding in Your fulness, Body, Blood, Soul and Divinity,
R. *have mercy on us.*
Jesus, Bread of Life,
R. *have mercy on us.*
Jesus, Bread of Angels,
R. *have mercy on us.*
Jesus, with us always until the end of the world,
R. *have mercy on us.*
Sacred Host, summit and source of all
worship and Christian life,
R. *have mercy on us.*
Sacred Host, sign and cause of the unity of the Church,
R. *have mercy on us.*
Sacred Host, adored by countless angels,
R. *have mercy on us.*
Sacred Host, spiritual food,
R. *have mercy on us.*

Sacred Host, Sacrament of love,
R. *have mercy on us.*
Sacred Host, bond of charity,
R. *have mercy on us.*
Sacred Host, greatest aid to holiness,
R. *have mercy on us.*
Sacred Host, gift and glory of the priesthood,
R. *have mercy on us.*
Sacred Host, in which we partake of Christ,
R. *have mercy on us.*
Sacred Host, in which the soul is filled with grace,
R. *have mercy on us.*
Sacred Host, in which we are given a pledge of future glory,
R. *have mercy on us.*

Blessed be Jesus in the Most Holy Sacrament of the Altar.
Blessed be Jesus in the Most Holy Sacrament of the Altar.
Blessed be Jesus in the Most Holy Sacrament of the Altar.
For those who do not believe in Your Eucharistic presence,
R. *have mercy, O Lord.*
For those who are indifferent to the Sacrament of Your love,
R. *have mercy on us.*
For those who have offended You in the Holy Sacrament of the Altar,
R. *have mercy on us.*
That we may show fitting reverence when entering Your holy temple,
R. *we beseech You, hear us.*
That we may make suitable preparation before approaching the Altar,
R. *we beseech You, hear us.*
That we may receive You frequently in Holy Communion with real devotion and true humility,
R. *we beseech You, hear us.*
That we may never neglect to thank You for so wonderful a blessing,
R. *we beseech You, hear us.*
That we may cherish time spent in silent prayer before You,
R. *we beseech You, hear us.*

That we may grow in knowledge of this Sacrament of sacraments,
R. *we beseech You, hear us.*
That all priests may have a profound love of the Holy Eucharist,
R. *we beseech You, hear us.*
That they may celebrate the Holy Sacrifice of the Mass in accordance with its sublime dignity,
R. *we beseech You, hear us.*
That we may be comforted and sanctified with Holy Viaticum at the hour of our death,
R. *we beseech You, hear us.*
That we may see You one day face to face in Heaven,
R. *we beseech You, hear us.*
Lamb of God, You take away the sins of the world,
R. *spare us, O Lord.*
Lamb of God, You take away the sins of the world,
R. *graciously hear us, O Lord.*
Lamb of God, You take away the sins of the world,
R. *have mercy on us, O Lord.*
V. O Sacrament Most Holy, O Sacrament Divine,
R. *all praise and all thanksgiving be every moment Thine.*

Let us pray,
Most merciful Father,
You continue to draw us to Yourself
through the Eucharistic Mystery.
Grant us fervent faith in this Sacrament of love,
in which Christ the Lord Himself is contained, offered and received.
We make this prayer through the same Christ our Lord.
R. Amen.[133]

---

[133] Description: Litany of the Blessed Sacrament: Written by Saint Peter Julian Eymard. This litany is ecclesiastically approved for liturgical use and has the Nihil Obstat and Imprimatur.

Litany to the Blessed Virgin Mary

Lord, *have mercy on us.*
Christ, *have mercy on us.*
Lord, *have mercy on us.*
Christ *hear us.*; Christ, *graciously hear us.*
God, the Father of Heaven, *have mercy on us.*
God, the Son, Redeemer of the world, *have mercy on us.*
God, the Holy Spirit, *have mercy on us.*
Holy Trinity, One God, *have mercy on us.*

Holy Mary, *pray for us.*
Holy Mother of God, *pray for us.*
Holy Virgin of virgins, *pray for us.*
Mother of Christ, *pray for us.*
Mother of divine grace, *pray for us.*
Mother most pure, *pray for us.*
Mother most chaste, *pray for us.*
Mother inviolate, *pray for us.*
Mother undefiled, *pray for us.*
Mother most amiable, *pray for us.*
Mother most admirable, *pray for us.*
Mother of good counsel, *pray for us.*
Mother of our Creator, *pray for us.*
Mother of our Savior, *pray for us.*
Virgin most prudent, *pray for us.*
Virgin most venerable, *pray for us.*
Virgin most renowned, *pray for us.*
Virgin most powerful, *pray for us.*
Virgin most merciful, *pray for us.*
Virgin most faithful, *pray for us.*
Mirror of justice, *pray for us.*
Seat of wisdom, *pray for us.*
Cause of our joy, *pray for us.*
Spiritual vessel, *pray for us.*
Vessel of honor, *pray for us.*
Singular vessel of devotion, *pray for us.*
Mystical rose, *pray for us.*

Tower of David, *pray for us.*
Tower of ivory, *pray for us.*
House of gold, *pray for us.*
Ark of the covenant, *pray for us.*
Gate of Heaven, *pray for us.*
Morning star, *pray for us.*
Health of the sick, *pray for us.*
Refuge of sinners, *pray for us.*
Comforter of the afflicted, *pray for us.*
Help of Christians, *pray for us.*
Queen of angels, *pray for us.*
Queen of patriarchs, *pray for us.*
Queen of prophets, *pray for us.*
Queen of apostles, *pray for us.*
Queen of martyrs, *pray for us.*
Queen of confessors, *pray for us.*
Queen of virgins, *pray for us.*
Queen of all saints, *pray for us.*
Queen conceived without Original Sin, *pray for us.*
Queen assumed into Heaven, *pray for us.*
Queen of the most holy Rosary, *pray for us.*
Queen of families, *pray for us.*
Queen of peace, *pray for us.*

Lamb of God, who takes away the sins of the world,
Spare us, O Lord.
Lamb of God, who takes away the sins of the world,
Graciously hear us O Lord.
Lamb of God, who takes away the sins of the world,
Have mercy on us.
V. Pray for us, O holy Mother of God.
R. *That we may be made worthy of the promises of Christ.*

Let us pray:
Grant, O Lord God, we beseech Thee, that we Thy servants may rejoice in continual health of mind and body; and, through the glorious intercession of Blessed Mary ever Virgin, may be freed from present sorrow, and enjoy eternal gladness. Through Christ our Lord. Amen.

REFERENCES

Eymard, St. Peter Julian. 1930. *Our Lady of The Blessed Sacrament.* Cleveland, Ohio: Emmanuel Publications.

—. 1990. *The Life and Letters of Saint Peter Julian Eymard, Volume 1: The Early Years 1828 - 1852.* Translated by Catherine Marie Caron, SSS. Cleveland: Congregation of the Blessed Sacrament.

Pelletier, SSS, Norman B. 2002. *Tomorrow Will Be Too Late: The Life of Saint Peter Julian Eymard, Apostle of the Eucharist.* Staten Island: Alba House.

Vaticana, Libreria Editrice. n.d. *Catechism of the Catholic Church, second edition.* United States Conference of Catholic Bishops. Kindle Edition.

Elisheba House

"By wisdom a house is built, by understanding it is established." (Proverbs 24:3)

Elisheba House is a Catholic media apostolate and company whose mission is to make known the love of God present in the Eucharist through the publishing of print and digital media and through several outreach programs, including conferences, presentations and retreats.

Visit us at:
www.elishebahouse.com

Sign up for our blog and journey with us as we strive to live a life centered in the Eucharist.

If you would like more information about
the Mothers of the Blessed Sacrament prayer cenacle,
you can email Laura Worhacz at:

Lauramay13mom@gmail.com